Diary of Samuel Pepys — Complete 1669 N.S. • Pepys, Samuel

Publisher's Note

Purchase of this book entitles you to a free trial membership in the publisher's book club at www.rarebooksclub.com. (Time limited offer.) Simply enter the barcode number from the back cover onto the membership form on our home page. The book club entitles you to select from millions of books at no additional charge. You can also download a digital copy of this and related books to read on the go. Simply enter the title or subject onto the search form to find them.

Note: This is an historic book. Pages numbers, where present in the text, refer to the first edition of the book and may also be in indexes.

If you have any questions, could you please be so kind as to consult our Frequently Asked Questions page at www.rarebooksclub.com/faqs.cfm? You are also welcome to contact us there.

Publisher: General Books LLC™, Memphis, TN, USA, 2012. ISBN: 9781153601290.

Proofreading: pgdp.net

CONTENTS

1668-1669 1
JANUARY 1668-1669 1
FEBRUARY 1668-1669 8
MARCH 1668-1669 16
APRIL 1669 28
MAY 1669 38

JANUARY 1668-1669

January 1st. Up, and presented from Captain Beckford with a noble silver warming-pan, which I am doubtful whether to take or no. Up, and with W. Hewer to the New Exchange, and then he and I to the cabinet-shops, to look out, and did agree, for a cabinet to give my wife for a New-year's gift; and I did buy one cost me L11, which is very pretty, of walnutt-tree, and will come home to-morrow. So back to the old Exchange, and there met my uncle Wight; and there walked, and met with the Houblons, and talked with them—gentlemen whom I honour mightily: and so to my uncle's, and met my wife; and there, with W. Hewer, we dined with our family, and had a very good dinner, and pretty merry and after dinner, my wife and I with our coach to the King's playhouse, and there in a box saw "The Mayden Queene." Knepp looked upon us, but I durst not shew her any countenance; and, as well as I could carry myself, I found my wife uneasy there, poor wretch! therefore, I shall avoid that house as much as I can. So back to my aunt's, and there supped and talked, and staid pretty late, it being dry and moonshine, and so walked home, and to bed in very good humour.

2nd. Up, at the office all the morning, and at noon home to dinner, where I find my cabinet come home, and paid for it, and it pleases me and my wife well. So after dinner busy late at the office, and so home and to bed.

3rd (Lord's day). Up, and busy all the morning, getting rooms and dinner ready for my guests, which were my uncle and aunt Wight, and two of their cousins, and an old woman, and Mr. Mills and his wife; and a good dinner, and all our plate out, and mighty fine and merry, only I a little vexed at burning a new table-cloth myself, with one of my trencher-salts. Dinner done, I out with W. Hewer and Mr. Spong, who by accident come to dine with me, and good talk with him: to White Hall by coach, and there left him, and I with my Lord Brouncker to attend the Duke of York, and then up and down the House till the evening, hearing how the King do intend this frosty weather, it being this day the first, and very hard frost, that hath come this year, and very cold it is. So home; and to supper and read; and there my wife and I treating about coming to an allowance to my wife for clothes; and there I, out of my natural backwardness, did hang off, which vexed her, and did occasion some discontented talk in bed, when we went to bed; and also in the morning, but I did recover all in the morning.

4th. Lay long, talking with my wife, and did of my own accord come to an allowance of her of L30 a-year for all expences, clothes and everything, which she was mightily pleased with, it being more than ever she asked or expected, and so rose, with much content, and up with W. Hewer to White Hall, there to speak with Mr. Wren, which I did about several things of the office entered in my memorandum books, and so about noon, going homeward with W. Hewer, he and I went in and saw the great tall woman that is to be seen, who is but twenty-one years old, and I do easily stand under her arms. Then, going further, The. Turner called me, out of her coach where her mother, &c., was, and invited me by all means to dine with them, at my cozen Roger's mistress's, the widow Dickenson! So, I went to them afterwards, and dined with them, and mighty handsomely treated, and she a wonderful merry, good-humoured, fat, but plain woman, but I believe a very good woman, and mighty civil to me. Mrs. Turner, the mother, and Mrs. Dyke, and The., and Betty was the company, and a gentleman of their acquaintance. Betty I did long to see, and she is indifferent pretty, but not what the world did speak of her; but I am mighty glad to have one so pretty of our kindred. After dinner, I walked with them, to shew them the great woman, which they admire, as well they may; and so back with them, and left them; and I to White Hall, where a Committee of Tangier met, but little to do there, but

I did receive an instance of the Duke of York's kindness to me, and the whole Committee, that they would not order any thing about the Treasurer for the Corporation now in establishing, without my assent, and considering whether it would be to my wrong or no. Thence up and down the house, and to the Duke of York's side, and there in the Duchess's presence; and was mightily complimented by my Lady Peterborough, in my Lord Sandwich's presence, whom she engaged to thank me for my kindness to her and her Lord. By and by I met my Lord Brouncker; and he and I to the Duke of York alone, and discoursed over the carriage of the present Treasurers, in opposition to, or at least independency of, the Duke of York, or our Board, which the Duke of York is sensible of, and all remember, I believe; for they do carry themselves very respectlessly of him and us. We also declared our minds together to the Duke of York about Sir John Minnes's incapacity to do any service in the Office, and that it is but to betray the King to have any business of trust committed to his weakness. So the Duke of York was very sensible of it and promised to speak to the King about it. That done, I with W. Hewer took up my wife at Unthank's, and so home, and there with pleasure to read and talk, and so to supper, and put into writing, in merry terms, our agreement between my wife and me, about L30 a-year, and so to bed. This was done under both our hands merrily, and put into W. Hewer's to keep.

5th. Up, and to the office all the morning, the frost and cold continuing. At noon home with my people to dinner; and so to work at the office again; in the evening comes Creed to me, and tells me his wife is at my house. So I in, and spent an hour with them, the first time she hath been here, or I have seen her, since she was married. She is not overhandsome, though a good lady, and one I love. So after some pleasant discourse, they gone, I to the Office again, and there late, and then home to supper to my wife, who is not very well of those, and so sat talking till past one in the morning, and then to bed.

6th (Twelfth day). Up, and to look after things against dinner to-day for my guests, and then to the Office to write down my journall for five or six days backward, and so home to look after dinner, it being now almost noon. At noon comes Mrs. Turner and Dyke, and Mrs. Dickenson, and then comes The. and Betty Turner, the latter of which is a very pretty girl; and then Creed and his wife, whom I sent for, by my coach. These were my guests, and Mrs. Turner's friend, whom I saw the other day, Mr. Wicken, and very merry we were at dinner, and so all the afternoon, talking, and looking up and down my house; and in the evening I did bring out my cake—a noble cake, and there cut it into pieces, with wine and good drink: and after a new fashion, to prevent spoiling the cake, did put so many titles into a hat, and so drew cuts; and I was the Queene; and The. Turner, King—Creed, Sir Martin Marr-all; and Betty, Mrs. Millicent: and so we were mighty merry till it was night; and then, being moonshine and fine frost, they went home, I lending some of them my coach to help to carry them, and so my wife and I spent the rest of the evening in talk and reading, and so with great pleasure to bed.

7th. Up, and to the office, where busy all the morning, and then at noon home to dinner, and thence my wife and I to the King's playhouse, and there saw "The Island Princesse," the first time I ever saw it; and it is a pretty good play, many good things being in it, and a good scene of a town on fire. We sat in an upper box, and the jade Nell come and sat in the next box; a bold merry slut, who lay laughing there upon people; and with a comrade of hers of the Duke's house, that come in to see the play. Thence home and to the office to do some business, and so home to supper and to bed.

8th. Up, and with Colonel Middleton, in his coach, and Mr. Tippets to White Hall; and there attended the Duke of York with the rest, where the Duke was mighty plain with the Treasurers, according to the advice my Lord Brouncker and I did give him the other night, and he did it fully; and so as, I believe, will make the Treasurers carefull of themselves, unless they do resolve upon defying the Duke of York. Thence with W. Hewer home, and to dinner, and so out again, my wife and I and Mr. Hater to White Hall, where she set us down, and she up and down to buy things, while we at the Treasury-Chamber, where I alone did manage the business of "The Leopard" against the whole Committee of the East India Company, with Mr. Blackburne with them; and to the silencing of them all, to my no great content. Thence walked to my wife, and so set out for home in our coach, it being very cold weather, and so to the office to do a little business, and then home to my wife's chamber, my people having laid the cloth, and got the rooms all clean above-stairs to-night for our dinner to-morrow, and therefore I to bed.

9th. Up, and at the office all the morning, and at noon, my Lord Brouncker, Mr. Wren, Joseph Williamson, and Captain Cocke, dined with me; and, being newly sat down, comes in, by invitation of Williamson's, the Lieutenant of the Tower, and he brings in with him young Mr. Whore, whose father, of the Tower, I know.— And here I had a neat dinner, and all in so good manner and fashion, and with so good company, and everything to my mind, as I never had more in my life— the company being to my heart's content, and they all well pleased. So continued, looking over my books and closet till the evening, and so I to the Office and did a good deal of business, and so home to supper and to bed with my mind mightily pleased with this day's management, as one of the days of my life of fullest content.

10th (Lord's day). Accidentally talking of our maids before we rose, I said a little word that did give occasion to my wife to fall out; and she did most vexatiously, almost all the morning, but ended most perfect good friends; but the thoughts of the unquiet which her ripping up of old faults will give me, did make me melancholy all day long. So about noon, past 12, we rose, and to dinner, and then to read and talk, my wife and I alone, for Balty was gone, who come to dine with us, and then in the evening comes Pelting to sit and talk with us, and so to supper and pretty merry discourse, only my mind a little vexed at the morning's work, but yet without any appearance. So after supper to bed.

11th. Up, and with W. Hewer, my guard, to White Hall, where no Committee of Tangier met, so up and down the House talking with this and that man, and so home, calling at the New Exchange for a book or two to send to Mr. Shepley and thence home, and thence to the 'Change, and there did a little business, and so walked home to dinner, and then abroad with my wife to the King's playhouse, and there saw "The Joviall Crew," but ill acted to what it was heretofore, in Clun's time, and when Lacy could dance. Thence to the New Exchange, to buy some things; and, among others, my wife did give me my pair of gloves, which, by contract, she is to give me in her L30 a-year. Here Mrs. Smith tells us of the great murder thereabouts, on Saturday last, of one Captain Bumbridge, by one Symons, both of her acquaintance; and hectors that were at play, and in drink: the former is killed, and is kinsman to my Lord of Ormond, which made him speak of it with so much passion, as I overheard him this morning, but could not make anything of it till now, but would they would kill more of them. So home; and there at home all the evening; and made Tom to prick down some little conceits and notions of mine, in musique, which do mightily encourage me to spend some more thoughts about it; for I fancy, upon good reason, that I am in the right way of unfolding the mystery of this matter, better than ever yet.

12th. Up, and to the Office, where, by occasion of a message from the Treasurers that their Board found fault with Commissioner Middleton, I went up from our Board to the Lords of the Treasury to meet our Treasurers, and did, and there did dispute the business, it being about the matter of paying a little money to Chatham Yard, wherein I find the Treasurers mighty supple, and I believe we shall bring them to reason, though they begun mighty upon us, as if we had no power of directing them, but they, us. Thence back presently home, to dinner, where I discern my wife to have been in pain about where I have been, but said nothing to me, but I believe did send W. Hewer to seek me, but I take no notice of it, but am vexed. So to dinner with my people, and then to the Office, where all the afternoon, and did much business, and at it late, and so home to supper, and to bed. This day, meeting Mr. Pierce at White Hall, he tells me that his boy hath a great mind to see me, and is going to school again; and Dr. Clerke, being by, do tell me that he is a fine boy; but I durst not answer anything, because I durst not invite him to my house, for fear of my wife; and therefore, to my great trouble, was forced to neglect that discourse. But here Mr. Pierce, I asking him whither he was going, told me as a great secret that he was going to his master's mistress, Mrs. Churchill, with some physic; meaning for the pox I suppose, or else that she is got with child. This evening I observed my wife mighty dull, and I myself was not mighty fond, because of some hard words she did give me at noon, out of a jealousy at my being abroad this morning, which, God knows, it was upon the business of the Office unexpectedly: but I to bed, not thinking but she would come after me. But waking by and by out of a slumber, which I usually fall into presently after my coming into the bed, I found she did not prepare to come to bed, but got fresh candles, and more wood for her fire, it being mighty cold, too. At this being troubled, I after a while prayed her to come to bed, all my people being gone to bed; so, after an hour or two, she silent, and I now and then praying her to come to bed, she fell out into a fury, that I was a rogue, and false to her. But yet I did perceive that she was to seek what to say, only she invented, I believe, a business that I was seen in a hackney coach with the glasses up with Deb., but could not tell the time, nor was sure I was he. I did, as I might truly, deny it, and was mightily troubled, but all would not serve. At last, about one o'clock, she come to my side of the bed, and drew my curtaine open, and with the tongs red hot at the ends, made as if she did design to pinch me with them, at which, in dismay, I rose up, and with a few words she laid them down; and did by little and, little, very sillily, let all the discourse fall; and about two, but with much seeming difficulty, come to bed, and there lay well all night, and long in bed talking together, with much pleasure, it being, I know, nothing but her doubt of my going out yesterday, without telling her of my going, which did vex her, poor wretch! last night, and I cannot blame her jealousy, though it do vex me to the heart.

13th. So up and by coach to Sir W. Coventry's, but he gone out, so I to White Hall, and thence walked out into the Park, all in the snow, with the Duke of York and the rest, and so home, after visiting my Lady Peterborough, and there by invitation find Mr. Povy, and there was also Talbot Pepys, newly come from Impington, and dined with me; and after dinner and a little talk with Povy about publick matters, he gone, and I and my wife and Talbot towards the Temple, and there to the King's playhouse, and there saw, I think, "The Maiden Queene," and so home and to supper and read, and to bed. This day come home the instrument I have so long longed for, the Parallelogram.

14th. Up and to the office, where all the morning busy, and so home to dinner, where Goodgroome with us, and after dinner a song, and then to the office, where busy till night, and then home to work there with W. Hewer to get ready some Tangier papers against to-morrow, and so to supper and to bed.

15th. Up, and by coach to Sir W. Coventry, where with him a good while in his chamber, talking of one thing or another; among others, he told me of the great factions at Court at this day, even to the sober engaging of great persons, and differences, and making the King cheap and ridiculous. It is about my Lady Harvy's being offended at Doll Common's acting of Sempronia, to imitate her; for which she got my Lord Chamberlain, her kinsman, to imprison Doll: when my Lady Castlemayne made the King to release her, and to order her to act it again, worse than ever, the other day, where the King himself was: and since it was acted again, and my Lady Harvy provided people to hiss her and fling oranges at her: but, it seems the heat is come to a great height, and real troubles at Court about it. Thence he and I out of doors, but he to Sir J. Duncomb, and I to White Hall through the Park, where I met the King and the Duke of York, and so walked with them, and so to White Hall, where the Duke of York met the office and did a little business; and I did give him thanks for his favour to me yesterday, at the Committee of Tangier, in my absence, Mr. Povy having given me advice of it, of the discourse there of doing something as to the putting the payment of the garrison into some undertaker's hand, Alderman Backewell, which the Duke of York would not suffer to go on, without my presence at the debate. And he answered me just thus: that he ought to have a care of him that do the King's business in the manner that I do, and words of more force than that. Then down with Lord Brouncker to Sir R. Murray, into the King's little elaboratory, under his closet, a pretty place; and there saw a great many chymical glasses and things, but understood none of them. So I home and to dinner, and then out again and stop with my wife at my cozen Turner's where I staid and sat a while, and carried The. and my wife to the Duke of York's house, to "Macbeth," and myself to White Hall, to the Lords of the Treasury, about Tangier business; and there was by at much merry discourse between them and my Lord Anglesey, who made sport of our new Treasurers, and called them his deputys, and much of that kind. And having done my own business, I away back, and carried my cozen Turner and sister Dyke to a friend's house, where they were to sup, in Lincoln's Inn Fields; and I to the Duke of York's house and saw the last two acts, and so carried The. thither, and so home with my wife, who read to me late, and so to supper and to bed. This day The. Turner shewed me at the play my Lady Portman, who has grown out of my knowledge.

16th. Up, and to the office all the morning, dined at home with my people, and so all the afternoon till night at the office busy, and so home to supper and to bed. This morning Creed, and in the afternoon comes Povy, to advise with me about my answer to the Lords [Commissioners] of Tangier, about the propositions for the Treasurership there, which I am not much concerned for. But the latter, talking of publick things, told me, as Mr. Wren also did, that the Parliament is likely to meets again, the King being frighted with what the Speaker hath put him in mind of—his promise not to prorogue, but only to adjourne them. They speak mighty freely of the folly of the King in this foolish woman's business, of my Lady Harvy. Povy tells me that Sir W. Coventry was with the King alone, an hour this day; and that my Lady Castlemayne is now in a higher command over the King than ever—not as a mistress, for she scorns him, but as a tyrant, to command him: and says that the Duchess of York and the Duke of York are mighty great with her, which is a great interest to my Lord Chancellor's' family; and that they do agree to hinder all they can the proceedings of the Duke of Buckingham and Arlington: and so we are in the old mad condition, or rather worse than any; no man knowing what the French intend to do the next summer.

17th (Lord's day). To church myself after seeing every thing fitted for dinner, and so, after church, home, and thither comes Mrs. Batelier and her two daughters to dinner to us; and W. Hewer and his mother, and Mr. Spong. We were very civilly merry, and Mrs. Batelier a very discreet woman, but mighty fond in the stories she tells of her son Will. After dinner, Mr. Spong and I to my closet, there to try my instrument Parallelogram, which do mighty well, to my full content; but only a little stiff, as being new. Thence, taking leave of my guests, he and I and W. Hewer to White Hall, and there parting with Spong, a man that I mightily love for his plainness and ingenuity, I into the Court, and there up and down and spoke with my Lords Bellassis and Peterborough about the business now in dispute, about my deputing a Treasurer to pay the garrison at Tangier, which I would avoid, and not be accountable, and they will serve me therein. Here I met Hugh May, and he brings me to the knowledge of Sir Henry Capell, a Member of Parliament, and brother of my Lord of Essex, who hath a great value, it seems, for me; and they appoint a day to come and dine with me, and see my books, and papers of the Office, which I shall be glad to shew them, and have opportunity to satisfy them therein. Here all the discourse is, that now the King is of opinion to have the Parliament called, notwithstanding his late resolutions for proroguing them; so unstable are his councils, and those about him. So staying late talking in the Queen's side, I away, with W. Hewer home, and there to read and talk with my wife, and so to bed.

18th. Up by candlelight, and with W. Hewer walked to the Temple, and thence took coach and to Sir William Coventry's, and there discoursed the business of my Treasurer's place, at Tangier, wherein he consents to my desire, and concurs therein, which I am glad of, that I may not be accountable for a man so far off. And so I to my Lord Sandwich's, and there walk with him through the garden, to White Hall, where he tells me what he had done about this Treasurer's place, and I perceive the whole thing did proceed from him: that finding it would be best to have the Governor have nothing to do with the pay of the garrison, he did propose to the Duke of York alone that a pay-master should be there; and that being desirous to do a courtesy to Sir Charles Harbord, and to prevent the Duke of York's looking out for any body else, he did name him to the Duke of York. That when he come the other day to move this to the Board of Tangier, the Duke of York, it seems, did readily reply, that it was fit to have Mr. Pepys satisfied therein first, and that it was not good to make places for persons. This my Lord in great confidence tells me, that he do take very ill from the Duke of York, though nobody knew the meaning of these words but him; and that he did take no notice of them, but bit his lip, being satisfied that the Duke of York's care of me was as desirable to him, as it could be to have Sir Charles Harbord: and did seem industrious to let me see that he was glad that the Duke of York and he might come to contend who shall be the kindest to me, which I owned as his great love, and so I hope and believe it is, though my Lord did go a little too far in this business, to move it so far, without consulting me. But I took no notice of that, but was glad to see this competition come about, that my Lord Sandwich is apparently jealous of my thinking that the Duke of York do mean me more kindness than him. So we walked together, and I took this occasion to invite him to dinner one day to my house, and he readily appointed Friday next, which I shall be glad to have over to his content, he having never yet eat a bit of my bread. Thence to the Duke of York on the King's side, with our Treasurers of the Navy, to discourse some business of the Navy, about the pay of the yards, and there I was taken notice of, many Lords being there in the room, of the Duke of York's conference with me; and so away, and meeting Mr. Sidney Montagu and Sheres, a small invitation served their turn to carry them to London, where I paid Sheres his L100, given him for his pains in drawing the plate of Tangier fortifications, &c., and so home to my house to dinner, where I had a pretty handsome sudden dinner, and all well pleased; and thence we three and my wife to the Duke of York's playhouse, and there saw "The Witts," a medley of things, but some similes mighty good, though ill mixed; and thence with my wife to the Exchange and bought some things, and so home, after I had been at White Hall, and there in the Queen's withdrawing-room invited my Lord Peterborough to dine with me, with my Lord Sandwich, who readily accepted it. Thence back and took up my wife at the 'Change, and so home. This day at noon I went with my young gentlemen (thereby to get a little time while W. Hewer went home to bid them get a dinner ready) to the Pope's Head tavern, there to see the fine painted room which Rogerson told me of, of his doing; but I do not like it at all, though it be good for such a publick room.

19th. Up, and at the office all the morning. At noon eat a mouthful, and so with my wife to Madam Turner's, and find her gone, but The. staid for us; and so to the King's house, to see "Horace;" this the third day of its acting—a silly tragedy; but Lacy hath made a farce of several dances—between each act, one: but his words are but silly, and invention not extraordinary, as to the dances; only some Dutchmen come out of the mouth and tail of a Hamburgh sow. Thence, not much pleased with the play, set them at home in the Strand; and my wife and I home, and there to do a little business at the Office, and so home to supper and to bed.

20th. Up; and my wife, and I, and W. Hewer to White Hall, where she set us down; and there I spoke with my Lord Peterborough, to tell him of the day for his dining with me being altered by my Lord Sandwich from Friday to Saturday next. And thence heard at the Council-board the City, by their single counsel Symson, and the company of Strangers Merchants, a debate the business of water-baylage; a tax demanded upon all goods, by the City, imported and exported: which these Merchants oppose, and demanding leave to try the justice of the City's demand by a Quo Warranto, which the City opposed, the Merchants did quite lay the City on their backs with great triumph, the City's cause being apparently too weak: but here I observed Mr. Gold, the merchant, to speak very well, and very sharply, against the City. Thence to my wife at Unthanke's, and with her and W. Hewer to Hercules Pillars, calling to do two or three things by the way, end there dined, and thence to the Duke of York's house, and saw "Twelfth Night," as it is now revived; but, I think, one of the weakest plays that ever I saw on the stage. This afternoon, before the play, I called with my wife at Dancre's, the great landscape-painter, by Mr. Povy's advice; and have bespoke him to come to take measure of my dining-room panels, and there I met with the pretty daughter of the coalseller's, that lived in Cheapside, and now in Covent Garden, who hath her picture drawn here, but very poorly; but she is a pretty woman, and now, I perceive, married, a very pretty black woman. So, the play done, we home, my wife letting fall some words of her observing my eyes to be mightily employed in the playhouse, meaning upon women, which did vex me; but, however, when we come home, we were good friends; and so to read, and to supper, and so to bed.

21st. Up, and walked to the Temple, it being frosty, and there took coach, my boy Tom with me, and so to White Hall to a Committee of Tangier, where they met, and by and by and till twelve at noon upon business, among others mine, where my desire about being eased of appointing and standing accountable for a Treasurer there was well accepted, and they will think of some other way. This I was glad of, finding reason to doubt that I might in this (since my Lord Sandwich made me understand what he had said to the Duke of York herein) fear to offend either the Duke of York by denying it, for he seemed on Sunday night last, when I first made known my desire to him herein to be a little amused at it, though I knew not then the reason, or else offend my Lord Sandwich by accepting it, or denying it in a manner that might not forward his desire for Sir Charles Harbord, but I thank God I did it to my great content without any offence, I think, to either. Thence in my own coach home, where I find Madam Turner, Dyke, and The., and had a good dinner for them, and merry; and so carried them to the Duke of York's house, all but Dyke, who went away on other business; and there saw "The Tempest;" but it is but ill done by Gosnell, in lieu of Moll Davis. Thence set them at home, and my wife and I to the 'Change, and so home, where my wife mighty dogged, and I vexed to see it, being mightily troubled, of late, at her being out of humour, for fear of her discovering any new matter of offence against me, though I am conscious of none; but do hate to be unquiet at home. So, late up, silent, and not supping, but hearing her utter some words of discontent to me with silence, and so to bed, weeping to myself for grief, which she discerning, come to bed, and mighty kind, and so with great joy on both sides to sleep.

22nd. Up, and with W. Hewer to White Hall, and there attended the Duke of York, and thence to the Exchange, in the way calling at several places on occasions relating to my feast to-morrow, on which my mind is now set; as how to get a new looking-glass for my dining-room, and some pewter, and good wine, against to-morrow; and so home, where I had the looking-glass set up, cost me L6 7s. 6d. And here at the 'Change I met with Mr. Dancre, the famous landscape painter, with whom I was on Wednesday; and he took measure of my panels in my dining-room, where, in the four, I intend to have the four houses of the King, White Hall, Hampton Court, Greenwich, and Windsor. He gone, I to dinner with my people, and so to my office to dispatch a little business, and then home to look after things against to-morrow, and among other things was mightily pleased with the fellow that come to lay the cloth, and fold the napkins, which I like so well, as that I am resolved to give him 40s. to teach my wife to do it. So to supper, with much kindness between me and my wife, which, now-a-days, is all my care, and so to bed.

23rd. Up, and again to look after the setting things right against dinner, which I did to very good content. So to the office, where all the morning till noon, when word brought me to the Board that my Lord Sandwich was come; so I presently rose, leaving the Board ready to rise, and there I found my Lord Sandwich, Peterborough, and Sir Charles Harbord; and presently after them comes my Lord Hinchingbroke, Mr. Sidney, and Sir William Godolphin. And after greeting them, and some time spent in talk, dinner was brought up, one dish after another, but a dish at a time, but all so good; but, above all things, the variety of wines, and excellent of their kind, I had for them, and all in so good order, that they were mightily pleased, and myself full of content at it: and indeed it was, of a dinner of about six or eight dishes, as noble as any man need to have, I think; at least, all was done in the noblest manner that ever I had any, and I have rarely seen in my life better anywhere else, even at the Court. After dinner, my Lords to cards, and the rest of us sitting about them and talking, and looking on my books and pictures, and my wife's drawings, which they commend mightily; and mighty merry all day long, with exceeding great content, and so till seven at night; and so took their leaves, it being dark and foul weather. Thus was this entertainment over, the best of its kind, and the fullest of honour and content to me, that ever I had in my life: and shall not easily have so good again. The truth is, I have some fear that I am more behind-hand in the world for these last two years, since I have not, or for some time could not, look after my accounts, which do a little allay my pleasure. But I do trust in God I am pretty well yet, and resolve, in a very little time, to look into my accounts, and see how they stand. So to my wife's chamber, and there supped, and got her cut my hair and look my shirt, for I have itched mightily these 6 or 7 days, and when all comes to all she finds that I am lousy, having found in my head and body about twenty lice, little and great, which I wonder at, being more than I have had I believe these 20 years. I did think I might have got them from the little boy, but they did presently look him, and found none. So how they come I know not, but presently did shift myself, and so shall be rid of them, and cut my hair close to my head, and so with much content to bed.

24th (Lord's day). An order brought me in bed, for the Principal Officers to attend the King at my Lord Keeper's this afternoon, it being resolved late the last night; and, by the warrant, I find my Lord Keeper did not then know the cause of it, the messenger being ordered to call upon him, to tell it him by the way, as he come to us. So I up, and to my Office to set down my Journall for yesterday, and so home, and with my wife to Church, and then home, and to dinner, and after dinner out with my wife by coach, to cozen Turner's, where she and The. gone to church, but I left my wife with Mrs. Dyke and Joyce Norton, whom I have not seen till now since their coming to town: she is become an old woman, and with as cunning a look as ever, and thence I to White Hall, and there walked up and down till the King and Duke of York were ready to go forth; and here I met Will. Batelier, newly come post from France, his boots all dirty. He brought letters to the King, and I glad to see him, it having been reported that he was drowned, for some days past, and then, he being gone, I to talk with Tom Killigrew, who told me and others, talking about the playhouse, that he is fain to keep a woman on purpose at 20s. a week to satisfy 8 or 10 of the young men of his house, whom till he did so he could never keep to their business, and now he do. By and by the King comes out, and so I took coach, and followed his coaches to my Lord Keeper's, at Essex House, where I never was before, since I saw my old Lord Essex lie in state when he was dead; a large, but ugly house. Here all the Officers of the Navy attended, and by and by were called in to the King and Cabinet, where my Lord, who was ill, did lie upon the bed, as my old Lord Treasurer, or Chancellor, heretofore used to; and the business was to know in what time all the King's ships might be repaired, fit for service. The Surveyor answered, in two years, and not sooner. I did give them hopes that, with supplies of money suitable, we might have them all fit for sea some part of the summer after this. Then they demanded in what time we could set out forty ships. It was answered, as they might be chosen of the newest and most ready, we could, with money, get forty ready against May. The King seemed mighty full that we should have money to do all that we desired, and satisfied that, without it, nothing could be done: and so, without determining any thing, we were dismissed; and I doubt all will end in some little fleete this year, and those of hired merchant-men, which would indeed be cheaper to the King, and have many conveniences attending it, more than to fit out the King's own; and this, I perceive, is designed, springing from Sir W. Coventry's counsel; and the King and most of the Lords, I perceive, full of it, to get the King's fleete all at once in condition for service. Thence I with Mr. Wren in his coach to my cozen Turner's for discourse sake, and in our way he told me how the business of the Parliament is wholly laid aside, it being overruled now, that they shall not meet, but must be prorogued, upon this argument chiefly, that all the differences between the two Houses, and things on foot, that were matters of difference and discontent, may be laid aside, and must begin again, if ever the House shall have a mind to pursue them. They must begin all anew. Here he set me down, and I to my cozen Turner, and stayed and talked a little; and so took my wife, and home, and there to make her read, and then to supper, and to bed. At supper come W. Batelier and supped with us, and told us many pretty things of France, and the greatness of the present King.

25th. Up, and to the Committee of Tangier, where little done, and thence I home by my own coach, and busy after dinner at my office all the afternoon till late at night, that my eyes were tired. So home, and my wife shewed me many excellent prints of Nanteuil's and others, which W. Batelier hath, at my desire, brought me out of France, of the King, and Colbert, and others, most excellent, to my great content. But he hath also brought a great many gloves perfumed, of several sorts; but all too big by half for her, and yet she will have two or three dozen of them, which vexed me, and made me angry. So she, at last, to please me, did come to take what alone I thought fit, which pleased me. So, after a little supper, to bed, my eyes being very bad.

26th. Up, and to the office, where busy sitting all the morning. Then to the Office again, and then to White Hall, leaving my wife at Unthanke's; and I to the Secretary's chamber, where I was, by particular order, this day summoned to attend, as I find Sir D. Gawden also was. And here was the King and the Cabinet met; and, being called in, among the rest I find my Lord Privy Seale, whom I never before knew to be in so much play, as to be of the Cabinet. The business is, that the Algerines have broke the peace with us, by taking some Spaniards and goods out of an English ship, which had the Duke of York's pass, of which advice come this day; and the King is resolved to stop Sir Thomas Allen's fleete from coming home till he hath amends made him for this affront, and therefore sent for us to advise about victuals to be sent to that fleete, and some more ships; wherein I answered them to what they demanded of me, which was but some few mean things; but I see that on all these occasions they seem to rely most upon me. And so, this being done, I took coach and took up my wife and straight home, and there late at the office busy, and then home, and there I find W. Batelier hath also sent the books which I made him bring me out of France. Among others, L'Estat, de France, Marnix, &c. , to my great content; and so I was well pleased with them, and shall take a time to look them over: as also one or two printed musick-books of songs; but my eyes are now too much out of tune to look upon them with any pleasure, therefore to supper and to bed.

27th. Up, and with Sir John Minnes in his coach to White Hall, where first we waited on the Lords of the Treasury about finishing the Victualling Contract; and there also I was put to it to make good our letter complaining against my Lord Anglesey's failing us in the payment of the moneys assigned us upon the Customs, where Mr. Fenn was, and I know will tell my Lord; but it is no matter, I am over shy already, and therefore must not fear. Then we up to a Committee of the Council for the Navy, about a business of Sir D. Gawden's relating to the Victualling, and thence I by hackney to the Temple to the Auditor's man, and with him to a tavern to meet with another under-auditor to advise about the clearing of my Lord Bellasses' accounts without injuring myself and perplexing my accounts, and so thence away to my cozen Turner's, where I find Roger Pepys come last night to town, and here is his mistress, Mrs. Dickenson, and by and by comes in Mr. Turner, a worthy, sober, serious man—I honour him mightily. And there we dined, having but an ordinary dinner; and so, after dinner, she, and I, and Roger, and his mistress, to the Duke of York's playhouse, and there saw "The Five Hours' Adventure," which hath not been acted a good while before, but once, and is a most excellent play, I must confess. My wife and The. come after us, after they had been to buy some things abroad, and so after the play done we to see them home, and then home ourselves, and my wife to read to me, and so to supper and to bed.

28th. Up, and to the office, where all the afternoon, also after dinner, and there late dispatching much business, and then home to supper with my wife, and to get her to read to me, and here I did find that Mr. Sheres hath, beyond his promise, not only got me a candlestick made me, after a form he remembers to have seen in Spain, for keeping the light from one's eyes, but hath got it done in silver very neat, and designs to give it me, in thanks for my paying him his L100 in money, for his service at Tangier, which was ordered him; but I do intend to force him to make me [pay] for it. But I yet, without his direction, cannot tell how it is to be made use of. So after a little reading to bed.

29th. Up, and with W. Hewer in Colonel Middleton's coach to White Hall, and there to the Duke of York, to attend him, where among other things I did give a severe account of our proceedings, and what we found, in the business of Sir W. Jenings's demand of Supernumeraries. I thought it a good occasion to make an example of him, for he is a proud, idle fellow; and it did meet with the Duke of York's acceptance and well-liking; and he did call him in, after I had done, and did not only give him a soft rebuke, but condemns him to pay both their victuals and wages, or right himself of the purser. This I was glad of, and so were all the rest of us, though I know I have made myself an immortal enemy by it. Thence home by hackney, calling Roger Pepys at the Temple gate in the bookseller's shop, and to the Old Exchange, where I staid a little to invite my uncle Wight, and so home, and there find my aunt Wight and her husband come presently, and so to dinner; and after dinner Roger, and I, and my wife, and aunt, to see Mr. Cole; but he nor his wife was within, but we looked upon his picture of Cleopatra, which I went principally to see, being so much commended by my wife and aunt; but I find it a base copy of a good originall, that vexed me to hear so much commended. Thence to see Creed's wife, and did so, and staid a while, where both of them within; and here I met Mr. Bland, newly come from Gales [Cadiz] after his differences with Norwood. I think him a foolish, light-headed man; but certainly he hath been abused in this matter by Colonel Norwood. Here Creed shewed me a copy of some propositions, which Bland and others, in the name of the Corporation of Tangier, did present to Norwood, for his opinion in, in order to the King's service, which were drawn up very humbly, and were really good things; but his answer to them was in the most shitten proud, carping, insolent, and ironically-prophane stile, that ever I saw in my life, so as I shall never think the place can do well, while he is there. Here, after some talk, and Creed's telling us that he is upon taking the next house to his present lodgings, which is next to that that my cozen Tom Pepys once lived in, in Newport Street, in Covent Garden; and is in a good place, and then, I suppose, he will keep his coach. So, setting Roger down at the Temple, who tells me that he is now concluded in all matters with his widow, we home, and there hired my wife to make an end of Boyle's Book of Formes, to-night and to-morrow; and so fell to read and sup, and then to bed. This day, Mr. Ned Pickering brought his lady to see my wife, in acknowledgment of a little present of oranges and olives, which I sent her, for his kindness to me in the buying of my horses, which was very civil. She is old, but hath, I believe, been a pretty comely woman:

30th. Lay long in bed, it being a fast-day for the murder of the late King; and so up and to church, where Dr. Hicks made a dull sermon; and so home, and there I find W. Batelier and Balty, and they dined with us, and I spent all the afternoon with my wife and W. Batelier talking, and then making them read, and particularly made an end of Mr. Boyle's Book of Formes, which I am glad to have over, and then fell to read a French discourse, which he hath brought over with him for me, to invite the people of France to apply themselves to Navigation, which it do very well, and is certainly their interest, and what will undo us in a few years, if the King of France goes on to fit up his Navy, and encrease it and his trade, as he hath begun. At night to supper, and after supper, and W. Batelier gone, my wife begun another book I lately bought, called "The State of England," which promises well, and is worth reading, and so after a while to bed.

31st (Lord's day). Lay long talking with pleasure, and so up and I to church, and there did hear the Doctor that is lately turned Divine, I have forgot his name, I met him a while since at Sir D. Gawden's at dinner, Dr. Waterhouse! He preaches in a devout manner of way, not elegant nor very persuasive, but seems to mean well, and that he would preach holily; and was mighty passionate against people that make a scoff of religion. And, the truth is, I did observe Mrs. Hollworthy smile often, and many others of the parish, who, I perceive, have known him, and were in mighty expectation of hearing him preach, but could not forbear smiling, and she particularly upon me, and I on her. So home to dinner: and before dinner to my Office, to set down my journal for this week, and then home to dinner; and after dinner to get my wife and boy, one after another, to read to me: and so spent the afternoon and the evening, and so after supper to bed. And thus endeth this month, with many different days of sadness and mirth, from differences between me and my wife, from her remembrance of my late unkindness to her with Willet, she not being able to forget it, but now and then hath her passionate remembrance of it as often as prompted to it by any occasion; but this night we are at present very kind. And so ends this month.

FEBRUARY 1668-1669

February 1st. Up, and by water from the Tower to White Hall, the first time that I have gone to that end of the town by water, for two or three months, I think, since I kept a coach, which God send propitious to me; but it is a very great convenience. I went to a Committee of Tangier, but it did not meet, and so I meeting Mr. Povy, he and I away to Dancre's, to speak something touching the pictures I am getting him to make for me. And thence he carried me to Mr. Streeter's, the famous history-painter over the way, whom I have often heard of, but did never see him before; and there I found him, and Dr. Wren, and several Virtuosos, looking upon the paintings which he is making for the new Theatre at Oxford: and, indeed, they look as if they would be very fine, and the rest think better than those of Rubens in the Banqueting-house at White Hall, but I do not so fully think so. But they will certainly be very noble; and I am mightily pleased to have the fortune to see this man and his work, which is very famous; and he a very civil little man, and lame, but lives very handsomely. So thence to my Lord Bellassis, and met him within: my business only to see a chimney-piece of Dancre's doing, in distemper, with egg to keep off the glaring of the light, which I must have done for my room: and indeed it is pretty, but, I must confess, I do think it is not altogether so beautiful as the oyle pictures; but I will have some of one, and some of another. Thence set him down at Little Turnstile, and so I home, and there eat a little dinner, and away with my wife by coach to the King's playhouse, thinking to have seen "The Heyresse," first acted on Saturday last; but when we come thither, we find no play there; Kinaston, that did act a part therein, in abuse to Sir Charles Sedley, being last night exceedingly beaten with sticks, by two or three that assaulted him, so as he is mightily bruised, and forced to keep his bed. So we to the Duke of York's playhouse, and there saw "She Would if She Could," and so home and to my office to business, and then to supper and to bed. This day, going to the play, The. Turner met us, and carried us to her mother, at my Lady Mordaunt's; and I did carry both mother and daughter with us to the Duke of York's playhouse, at next door.

2nd. Up, and to the office, where all the morning, and home to dinner at noon, where I find Mr. Sheres; and there made a short dinner, and carried him with us to the King's playhouse, where "The Heyresse," not-withstanding Kinaston's being beaten, is acted; and they say the King is very angry with Sir Charles Sedley for his being beaten, but he do deny it. But his part is done by Beeston, who is fain to read it out of a book all the while, and thereby spoils the part, and almost the play, it being one of the best parts in it; and though the design is, in the first conception of it, pretty good, yet it is but an indifferent play, wrote, they say, by my Lord Newcastle. But it was pleasant to see Beeston come in with others, supposing it to be dark, and yet he is forced to read his part by the light of the candles: and this I observing to a gentleman that sat by me, he was mightily pleased therewith, and spread it up and down. But that, that pleased me most in the play is, the first song that Knepp sings, she singing three or four; and, indeed, it was very finely sung, so as to make the whole house clap her. Thence carried Sheres to White Hall, and there I stepped in, and looked out Mr. May, who tells me that he and his company cannot come to dine with me to-morrow, whom I expected only to come to see the manner of our Office and books, at which I was not very much displeased, having much business at the Office, and so away home, and there to the office about my letters, and then home to supper and to bed, my wife being in mighty ill humour all night, and in the morning I found it to be from her observing Knepp to wink and smile on me; and she says I smiled on her; and, poor wretch! I did perceive that she did, and do on all such occasions, mind my eyes. I did, with much difficulty, pacify her, and were friends, she desiring that hereafter, at that house, we might always sit either above in a box, or, if there be [no] room, close up to the lower boxes.

3rd. So up, and to the Office till noon, and then home to a little dinner, and thither again till night, mighty busy, to my great content, doing a great deal of business, and so home to supper, and to bed; I finding this day that I may be able to do a great deal of business by dictating, if I do not read myself, or write, without spoiling my eyes, I being very well in my eyes after a great day's work.

4th. Up, and at the office all the morning. At noon home with my people to dinner, and then after dinner comes Mr. Spong to see me, and brings me my Parallelogram, in better order than before, and two or three draughts of the port of Brest, to my great content, and I did call Mr. Gibson to take notice of it, who is very much pleased therewith; and it seems this Parallelogram is not, as Mr. Sheres would, the other day, have persuaded me, the same as a Protractor, which do so much the more make me value it, but of itself it is a most usefull instrument. Thence out with my wife and him, and carried him to an instrument-maker's shop in Chancery Lane, that was once a 'Prentice of Greatorex's, but the master was not within, and there he [Gibson] shewed me a Parallelogram in brass, which I like so well that I will buy, and therefore bid it be made clean and fit for me. And so to my cozen Turner's, and there just spoke with The., the mother not being at home; and so to the New Exchange, and thence home to my letters; and so home to supper and to bed. This morning I made a slip from the Office to White Hall, expecting Povy's business at a Committee of Tangier, at which I would be, but it did not meet, and so I presently back.

5th. Up betimes, by coach to Sir W. Coventry's, and with him by coach to White Hall, and there walked in the garden talking of several things, and by my visit to keep fresh my interest in him; and there he tells me how it hath been talked that he was to go one of the Commissioners to Ireland, which he was resolved never to do, unless directly commanded; for he told me that for to go thither, while the Chief Secretary of State was his professed enemy, was to undo himself; and, therefore, it were better for him to venture being unhappy here, than to go further off, to be undone by some obscure instructions, or whatever other way of mischief his enemies should cut out for him. He mighty kind to me, and so parted, and thence home, calling in two or three places—among others, Dancre's, where I find him beginning of a piece for me, of Greenwich, which will please me well, and so home to dinner, and very busy all the afternoon, and so at night home to supper, and to bed.

6th. Up, and to the office, where all the morning, and thence after dinner to the King's playhouse, and there,—in an upper box, where come in Colonel Poynton and Doll Stacey, who is very fine, and, by her wedding-ring, I suppose he hath married her at last,—did see "The Moor of Venice:" but ill acted in most parts; Mohun, which did a little surprise me, not acting Iago's part by much so well as Clun used to do; nor another Hart's, which was Cassio's; nor, indeed, Burt doing the Moor's so well as I once thought he did. Thence home, and just at Holborn Conduit the bolt broke, that holds the fore-wheels to the perch, and so the horses went away with them, and left the coachman and us; but being near our coachmaker's, and we staying in a little ironmonger's shop, we were presently supplied with another, and so home, and there to my letters at the office, and so to supper and to bed.

7th (Lord's day). My wife mighty peevish in the morning about my lying unquietly a-nights, and she will have it that it is a late practice, from my evil thoughts in my dreams,.and mightily she is troubled about it; but all blew over, and I up, and to church, and so home to dinner, where she in a worse fit, which lasted all the afternoon, and shut herself up, in her closet, and I mightily grieved and vexed, and could not get her to tell me what ayled her, or to let me into her closet, but at last she did, where I found her crying on the ground, and I could not please her; but I did at last find that she did plainly expound it to me. It was, that she did believe me false to her with Jane, and did rip up three or four silly circumstances of her not rising till I come out of my chamber, and her letting me thereby see her dressing herself; and that I must needs go into her chamber and was naught with her; which was so silly, and so far from truth, that I could not be troubled at it, though I could not wonder at her being troubled, if she had these thoughts, and therefore she would lie from me, and caused sheets to be put on in the blue room, and would have Jane to lie with her lest I should come to her. At last, I did give her such satisfaction, that we were mighty good friends, and went to bed betimes .

8th. Up, and dressed myself; and by coach, with W. Hewer and my wife, to White Hall, where she set us two down; and in the way, our little boy, at Martin, my bookseller's shop, going to 'light, did fall down; and, had he not been a most nimble boy (I saw how he did it, and was mightily pleased with him for it), he had been run over by the coach. I to visit my Lord Sandwich; and there, while my Lord was dressing himself, did see a young Spaniard, that he hath brought over with him, dance, which he is admired for, as the best dancer in Spain, and indeed he do with mighty mastery; but I do not like his dancing as the English, though my Lord commends it mightily: but I will have him to my house, and show it my wife. Here I met with Mr. Moore, who tells me the state of my Lord's accounts of his embassy, which I find not so good as I thought: for, though it be passed the King and his Cabal (the Committee for Foreign Affairs as they are called), yet they have cut off from L9000 full L8000, and have now sent it to the Lords of the Treasury, who, though the Committee have allowed the rest, yet they are not obliged to abide by it. So that I do fear this account may yet be long ere it be passed—much more, ere that sum be paid: I am sorry for the family, and not a little for what it owes me. So to my wife, took her up at Unthank's, and in our way home did shew her the tall woman in Holborne, which I have seen before; and I measured her, and she is, without shoes, just six feet five inches high, and they say not above twenty-one years old. Thence home, and there to dinner, and my wife in a wonderful ill humour; and, after dinner, I staid with her alone, being not able to endure this life, and fell to some angry words together; but by and by were mighty good friends, she telling me plain it was still about Jane, whom she cannot believe but I am base with, which I made a matter of mirth at; but at last did call up Jane, and confirm her mistress's directions for her being gone at Easter, which I find the wench willing to be, but directly prayed that Tom might go with her, which I promised, and was but what I designed; and she being thus spoke with, and gone, my wife and I good friends, and mighty kind, I having promised, and I will perform it, never to give her for the time to come ground of new trouble; and so I to the Office, with a very light heart, and there close at my business all the afternoon. This day I was told by Mr. Wren, that Captain Cox, Master-Attendant at Deptford, is to be one of us very soon, he and Tippets being to take their turns for Chatham and Portsmouth, which choice I like well enough; and Captain Annesley is to come in his room at Deptford. This morning also, going to visit Roger Pepys, at the potticary's in King's Street, he tells me that Roger is gone to his wife's, so that they have been married, as he tells me, ever since the middle of last week: it was his design, upon good reasons, to make no noise of it; but I am well enough contented that it is over. Dispatched a great deal of business at the office, and there pretty late, till finding myself very full of wind, by my eating no dinner to-day, being vexed, I was forced to go home, and there supped W. Batelier with us, and so with great content to bed.

9th. Up, and all the morning busy at the office, and after dinner abroad with my wife to the King's playhouse, and there saw "The Island Princesse," which I like mighty well, as an excellent play: and here we find Kinaston to be well enough to act again, which he do very well, after his beating by Sir Charles Sedley's appointment; and so thence home, and there to my business at the Office, and after my letters done, then home to supper and to bed, my mind being mightily eased by my having this morning delivered to the Office a letter of advice about our answers to the Commissioners of Accounts, whom we have neglected, and I have done this as a record in my justification hereafter, when it shall come to be examined.

10th. Up, and with my wife and W. Hewer, she set us down at White Hall, where the Duke of York was gone a-hunting: and so, after I had done a little business there, I to my wife, and with her to the plaisterer's at Charing Cross, that casts heads and bodies in plaister: and there I had my whole face done; but I was vexed first to be forced to daub all my face over with pomatum: but it was pretty to feel how soft and easily it is done on the face, and by and by, by degrees, how hard it becomes, that you cannot break it, and sits so close, that you cannot pull it off, and yet so easy, that it is as soft as a pillow, so safe is everything where many parts of the body do bear alike. Thus was the mould made; but when it came off there was little pleasure in it, as it looks in the mould, nor any resemblance whatever there will be in the figure, when I come to see it cast off, which I am to call for a day or two hence, which I shall long to see. Thence to Hercules Pillars, and there my wife and W. Hewer and I dined, and back to White Hall, where I staid till the Duke of York come from hunting, which he did by and by, and, when dressed, did come out to dinner; and there I waited: and he did tell me that to-morrow was to be the great day that the business of the Navy would be discoursed of before the King and his Caball, and that he must stand on his guard, and did design to have had me in readiness by, but that upon second thoughts did think it better to let it alone, but they are now upon entering into the economical part of the Navy. Here he dined, and did mightily magnify his sauce, which he did then eat with every thing, and said it was the best universal sauce in the world, it being taught him by the Spanish Embassador; made of some parsley and a dry toast, beat in a mortar, together with vinegar, salt, and a little pepper: he eats it with flesh, or fowl, or fish: and then he did now mightily commend some new sort of wine lately found out, called Navarre wine, which I tasted, and is, I think, good wine: but I did like better the notion of the sauce, and by and by did taste it, and liked it mightily. After dinner, I did what I went for, which was to get his consent that Balty might hold his Muster-Master's place by deputy, in his new employment which I design for him, about the Storekeeper's accounts; which the Duke of York did grant me, and I was mighty glad of it. Thence home, and there I find Povy and W. Batelier, by appointment, met to talk of some merchandize of wine and linnen; but I do not like of their troubling my house to meet in, having no mind to their pretences of having their rendezvous here, but, however, I was not much troubled, but went to the office, and there very busy, and did much business till late at night, and so home to supper, and with great pleasure to bed. This day, at dinner, I sent to Mr. Spong to come to me to Hercules Pillars, who come to us, and there did bring with him my new Parallelogram of brass, which I was mightily pleased with, and paid for it 25s., and am mightily pleased with his ingenious and modest company.

11th. Up, and to the office, where sat all the morning, and at noon home and heard that the last night Colonel Middleton's wife died, a woman I never saw since she come hither, having never been within their house since. Home at noon to dinner, and thence to work all the afternoon with great pleasure, and did bring my business to a very little compass in my day book, which is a mighty pleasure, and so home to supper and get my wife to read to me, and then to bed.

12th. Up, and my wife with me to White Hall, and Tom, and there she sets us down, and there to wait on the Duke of York, with the rest of us, at the Robes, where the Duke of York did tell us that the King would have us prepare a draught of the present administration of the Navy, and what it was in the late times, in order to his being able to distinguish between the good and the bad, which I shall do, but to do it well will give me a great deal of trouble. Here we shewed him Sir J. Minnes's propositions about balancing Storekeeper's accounts; and I did shew him Hosier's, which did please him mightily, and he will have it shewed the Council and King anon, to be put in practice. Thence to the Treasurer's; and I and Sir J. Minnes and Mr. Tippets down to the Lords Commissioners of the Treasury, and there had a hot debate from Sir Thomas Clifford and my Lord Ashly (the latter of which, I hear, is turning about as fast as he can to the Duke of Buckingham's side, being in danger, it seems, of being otherwise out of play, which would not be convenient for him), against Sir W. Coventry and Sir J. Duncomb, who did uphold our Office against an accusation of our Treasurers, who told the Lords that they found that we had run the King in debt L50,000 or more, more than the money appointed for the year would defray, which they declared like fools, and with design to hurt us, though the thing is in itself ridiculous. But my Lord Ashly and Clifford did most horribly cry out against the want of method in the Office. At last it come that it should be put in writing what they had to object; but I was devilish mad at it, to see us thus wounded by our own members, and so away vexed, and called my wife, and to Hercules Pillars, Tom and I, there dined; and here there coming a Frenchman by with his Shew, we did make him shew it us, which he did just as Lacy acts it, which made it mighty pleasant to me. So after dinner we away and to Dancre's, and there saw our picture of Greenwich in doing, which is mighty pretty, and so to White Hall, my wife to Unthank's, and I attended with Lord Brouncker the King and Council, about the proposition of balancing Storekeeper's accounts and there presented Hosier's book, and it was mighty well resented and approved of. So the Council being up, we to the Queen's side with the King and Duke of York: and the Duke of York did take me out to talk of our Treasurers, whom he is mighty angry with: and I perceive he is mighty desirous to bring in as many good motions of profit and reformation in the Navy as he can, before the Treasurers do light upon them, they being desirous, it seems, to be thought the great reformers: and the Duke of York do well. But to my great joy he is mighty open to me in every thing; and by this means I know his whole mind, and shall be able to secure myself, if he stands. Here to-night I understand, by my Lord Brouncker, that at last it is concluded on by the King and Buckingham that my Lord of Ormond shall not hold his government of Ireland, which is a great stroke, to shew the power of Buckingham and the poor spirit of the King, and little hold that any man can have of him. Thence I homeward, and calling my wife called at my cozen Turner's, and there met our new cozen Pepys (Mrs. Dickenson), and Bab. and Betty' come yesterday to town, poor girls, whom we have reason to love, and mighty glad we are to see them; and there staid and talked a little, being also mightily pleased to see Betty Turner, who is now in town, and her brothers Charles and Will, being come from school to see their father, and there talked a while, and so home, and there Pelling hath got me W. Pen's book against the Trinity.

[Entitled, "The Sandy Foundation

Shaken; or those. doctrines of one God subsisting in three distinct and separate persons; the impossibility of God's pardoning sinners without a plenary satisfaction, the justification of impure persons by an imputative righteousness, refuted from the authority of Scripture testimonies and right reason, etc. London, 1668. " It caused him to be imprisoned in the Tower. "Aug. 4, 1669. Young Penn who wrote the blasphemous book is delivered to his father to be transported" ("Letter to Sir John Birkenhead, quoted by Bishop Kennett in his MS. Collections, vol. lxxxix., p. 477).]

I got my wife to read it to me; and I find it so well writ as, I think, it is too good for him ever to have writ it; and it is a serious sort of book, and not fit for every body to read. So to supper and to bed.

13th. Up, and all the morning at the office, and at noon home to dinner, and thence to the office again mighty busy, to my great content, till night, and then home to supper and, my eyes being weary, to bed.

14th (Lord's day). Up, and by coach to Sir W. Coventry, and there, he taking physic, I with him all the morning, full of very good discourse of the Navy and publick matters, to my great content, wherein I find him doubtful that all will be bad, and, for his part, he tells me he takes no more care for any thing more than in the Treasury; and that, that being done, he goes to cards and other delights, as plays, and in summertime to bowles. But here he did shew me two or three old books of the Navy, of my Lord Northumberland's' times, which he hath taken many good notes out of, for justifying the Duke of York and us, in many things, wherein, perhaps, precedents will be necessary to produce, which did give me great content. At noon home, and pleased mightily with my morning's work, and coming home, I do find a letter from Mr. Wren, to call me to the Duke of York after dinner. So dined in all haste, and then W. Hewer and my wife and I out, we set her at my cozen Turner's while we to White Hall, where the Duke of York expected me; and in his closet Wren and I. He did tell me how the King hath been acquainted with the Treasurers' discourse at the Lords Commissioners of the Treasury, the other day, and is dissatisfied with our running him in debt, which I removed; and he did, carry me to the King, and I did satisfy him also; but his satisfaction is nothing worth, it being easily got, and easily removed; but I do purpose to put in writing that which shall make the Treasurers ashamed. But the Duke of York is horrid angry against them; and he hath cause, for they do all they can to bring dishonour upon his management, as do vainly appear in all they do. Having done with the Duke of York, who do repose all in me, I with Mr. Wren to his, chamber, to talk; where he observed, that these people are all of them a broken sort of people, that have not much to lose, and therefore will venture all to make their fortunes better: that Sir Thomas Osborne is a beggar, having 11 of L1200 a-year, but owes above L10,000. The Duke of Buckingham's condition is shortly this: that he hath about L19,600 a-year, of which he pays away about L7,000 a-year in interest, about L2000 in fee-farm rents to the King, about L6000 wages and pensions, and the rest to live upon, and pay taxes for the whole. Wren says, that for the Duke of York to stir in this matter, as his quality might justify, would but make all things worse, and that therefore he must bend, and suffer all, till time works it out: that he fears they will sacrifice the Church, and that the King will take anything, and so he will hold up his head a little longer, and then break in pieces. But Sir W. Coventry did today mightily magnify my late Lord Treasurer, for a wise and solid, though infirm man: and, among other things, that when he hath said it was impossible in nature to find this or that sum of money, and my Lord Chancellor hath made sport of it, and tell the King that when my Lord hath said it [was] impossible, yet he hath made shift to find it, and that was by Sir G. Carteret's getting credit, my Lord did once in his hearing say thus, which he magnifies as a great saying—that impossible would be found impossible at last; meaning that the King would run himself out, beyond all his credit and funds, and then we should too late find it impossible; which is, he says, now come to pass. For that Sir W. Coventry says they could borrow what money they would, if they had assignments, and funds to secure it with, which before they had enough of, and then must spend it as if it would never have an end. From White Hall to my cozen Turner's, and there took up my wife; and so to my uncle Wight's, and there sat and supped, and talked pretty merry, and then walked home, and to bed.

15th. Up, and with Tom to White Hall; and there at a Committee of Tangier, where a great instance of what a man may lose by the neglect of a friend: Povy never had such an opportunity of passing his accounts, the Duke of York being there, and everybody well disposed, and in expectation of them; but my Lord Ashly, on whom he relied, and for whose sake this day was pitched on, that he might be sure to be there, among the rest of his friends, staid too long, till the Duke of York and the company thought unfit to stay longer and so the day lost, and God knows when he will ever have so good a one again, as long as he lives; and this was the man of the whole company that he hath made the most interest to gain, and now most depended upon him. So up and down the house a while, and then to the plaisterer's, and there saw the figure of my face taken from the mould: and it is most admirably like, and I will have another made, before I take it away, and therefore I away and to the Temple, and thence to my cozen Turner's, where, having the last night been told by her that she had drawn me for her Valentine, I did this day call at the New Exchange, and bought her a pair of green silk stockings and garters and shoe-strings, and two pair of jessimy gloves, all coming to about 28s., and did give them her this noon. At the 'Change, I did at my bookseller's shop accidentally fall into talk with Sir Samuel Tuke about trees, and Mr. Evelyn's garden; and I do find him, I think, a little conceited, but a man of very fine discourse as any I ever heard almost, which I was mighty glad of. I dined at my cozen Turner's, and my wife also and her husband there, and after dinner, my wife and I endeavoured to make a visit to Ned Pickering; but he not at home, nor his lady; and therefore back again, and took up my cozen Turner, and to my cozen Roger's lodgings, and there find him pretty well again, and his wife mighty kind and merry, and did make mighty much of us, and I believe he is married to a very good woman. Here was also Bab. and Betty, who have not their clothes yet, and therefore cannot go out, otherwise I would have had them abroad to-morrow; but the poor girls mighty kind to us, and we must skew them kindness also. Here in Suffolk Street lives Moll Davis; and we did see her coach come for her to her door, a mighty pretty fine coach. Here we staid an hour or two, and then carried Turner home, and there staid and talked a while, and then my wife and I to White Hall; and there, by means of Mr. Cooling, did get into the play, the only one we have seen this winter: it was "The Five Hours' Adventure:" but I sat so far I could not hear well, nor was there any pretty woman that I did see, but my wife, who sat in my Lady Fox's pew

[We may suppose that pews were by no means common at this time
 within consecrated walls, from the word being applied indifferently
 by Pepys to a box in a place of amusement, and two days afterwards
 to a seat at church. It would appear, from other authorities, that
 between 1646 and 1660 scarcely any pews had been erected; and Sir C.
 Wren is known to have objected to their introduction into his London
 churches.—B.]

with her. The house very full; and late before done, so that it was past eleven before we got home. But we were well pleased with seeing it, and so to supper, where it happened that there was no bread in the house, which was an unusual case, and so to bed.

16th. Up, and to the office, where all the morning, my head full of business of the office now at once on my hands, and so at noon home to dinner, where I find some things of W. Batelier's come out of France, among which some clothes for my wife, wherein she is likely to lead me to the expence of so much money as vexed me; but I seemed so, more than I at this time was, only to prevent her taking too much, and she was mighty calm under it. But I was mightily pleased with another picture of the King of France's head, of Nanteuil's, bigger than the other which he brought over, that pleases me infinitely: and so to the Office, where busy all the afternoon, though my eyes mighty bad with the light of the candles last night, which was so great as to make my eyes sore all this day, and do teach me, by a manifest experiment, that it is only too much light that do make my eyes sore. Nevertheless, with the help of my tube, and being desirous of easing my mind of five or six days journall, I did venture to write it down from ever since this day se'nnight, and I think without hurting my eyes any more than they were before, which was very much, and so home to supper and to bed.

17th. Up, and with W. Hewer with me to Lincoln's Inn, by appointment, to have spoke with Mr. Pedley about Mr. Goldsborough's business and Mr. Weaver's, but he was gone out, and so I with Mr. Castle, the son-in-law of Weaver, to White Hall to look for him, but did not find him, but here I did meet with several and talked, and do hear only that the King dining yesterday at the Dutch Embassador's, after dinner they drank, and were pretty merry; and, among the rest of the King's company, there was that worthy fellow my lord of Rochester, and Tom Killigrew, whose mirth and raillery offended the former so much, that he did give Tom Killigrew a box on the ear in the King's presence, which do much give offence to the people here at Court, to see how cheap the King makes himself, and the more, for that the King hath not only passed by the thing, and pardoned it to Rochester already, but this very morning the King did publickly walk up and down, and Rochester I saw with him as free as ever, to the King's everlasting shame, to have so idle a rogue his companion. How Tom Killigrew takes it, I do not hear. I do also this day hear that my Lord Privy Seale do accept to go Lieutenant into Ireland; but whether it be true or no, I cannot tell. So calling at my shoemaker's, and paying him to this day, I home to dinner, and in the afternoon to Colonel Middleton's house, to the burial of his wife, where we are all invited, and much more company, and had each of us a ring: and so towards evening to our church, where there was a sermon preached by Mills, and so home. At church there was my Lord Brouncker and Mrs. Williams in our pew, the first time they were ever there or that I knew that either of them would go to church. At home comes Castle to me, to desire me to go to Mr. Pedly, this night, he being to go out of town to-morrow morning, which I, therefore, did, by hackney-coach, first going to White Hall to meet with Sir W. Coventry, but missed him. But here I had a pleasant rencontre of a lady in mourning, that, by the little light I had, seemed handsome. I passing by her, I did observe she looked back again and again upon me, I suffering her to go before, and it being now duske. I observed she went into the little passage towards the Privy Water-Gate, and I followed, but missed her; but coming back again, I observed she returned, and went to go out of the Court. I followed her, and took occasion, in the new passage now built, where the walke is to be, to take her by the hand, to lead her through, which she willingly accepted, and I led her to the Great Gate, and there left her, she telling me, of her own accord, that she was going as far as, Charing Cross; but my boy was at the gate, and so je durst not go out con her, which vexed me, and my mind (God forgive me) did run apres her toute that night, though I have reason to thank God, and so I do now, that I was not tempted to go further. So to Lincoln's Inn, where to

Mr. Pedly, with whom I spoke, and did my business presently: and I find him a man of very good language, and mighty civil, and I believe very upright: and so home, where W. Batelier was, and supped with us, and I did reckon this night what I owed him; and I do find that the things my wife, of her own head, hath taken (together with my own, which comes not to above L5), comes to above L22. But it is the last, and so I am the better contented; and they are things that are not trifles, but clothes, gloves, shoes, hoods, &c. So after supper, to bed.

18th. Up, and to the Office, and at noon home, expecting to have this day seen Bab. and Betty Pepys here, but they come not; and so after dinner my wife and I to the Duke of York's house, to a play, and there saw "The Mad Lover," which do not please me so well as it used to do, only Betterton's part still pleases me. But here who should we have come to us but Bab. and Betty and Talbot, the first play they were yet at; and going to see us, and hearing by my boy, whom I sent to them, that we were here, they come to us hither, and happened all of us to sit by my cozen Turner and The., and we carried them home first, and then took Bab. and Betty to our house, where they lay and supped, and pretty merry, and very fine with their new clothes, and good comely girls they are enough, and very glad I am of their being with us, though I would very well have been contented to have been without the charge. So they to bed and we to bed.

19th. Up, and after seeing the girls, who lodged in our bed, with their maid Martha, who hath been their father's maid these twenty years and more, I with Lord Brouncker to White Hall, where all of us waited on the Duke of York; and after our usual business done, W. Hewer and I to look my wife at the Black Lion, Mercer's, but she is gone home, and so I home and there dined, and W. Batelierand W. Hewer with us. All the afternoon I at the Office, while the young people went to see Bedlam, and at night home to them and to supper, and pretty merry, only troubled with a great cold at this time, and my eyes very bad ever since Monday night last that the light of the candles spoiled me. So to bed. This morning, among other things, talking with Sir W. Coventry, I did propose to him my putting in to serve in Parliament, if there should, as the world begins to expect, be a new one chose: he likes it mightily, both for the King's and Service's sake, and the Duke of York's, and will propound it to the Duke of York: and I confess, if there be one, I would be glad to be in.

20th. Up, and all the morning at the office, and then home to dinner, and after dinner out with my wife and my two girls to the Duke of York's house, and there saw "The Gratefull Servant," a pretty good play, and which I have forgot that ever I did see. And thence with them to Mrs. Gotier's, the Queen's tire-woman, for a pair of locks for my wife; she is an oldish French woman, but with a pretty hand as most I have seen; and so home, and to supper, W. Batelier and W. Hewer with us, and so my cold being great, and greater by my having left my coat at my tailor's tonight and come home in a thinner that I borrowed there, I went to bed before them and slept pretty well.

21st (Lord's day). Up, and with my wife and two girls to church, they very fine; and so home, where comes my cozen Roger and his wife, I having sent for them, to dine with us, and there comes in by chance also Mr. Shepley, who is come to town with my Lady Paulina, who is desperately sick, and is gone to Chelsey, to the old house where my Lord himself was once sick, where I doubt my Lord means to visit hers more for young Mrs. Beck's sake than for hers. Here we dined with W. Batelier, and W. Hewer with us, these two, girls making it necessary that they be always with us, for I am not company light enough to be always merry with them and so sat talking all the afternoon, and then Shepley went: away first, and then my cozen Roger and his wife. And so I, to my Office, to write down my Journall, and so home to my chamber and to do a little business there, my papers being in mighty disorder, and likely so to continue while these girls are with us. In the evening comes W. Batelier and his sisters and supped and talked with us, and so spent the evening, myself being somewhat out of order because of my eyes, which have never been well since last Sunday's reading at Sir W. Coventry's chamber, and so after supper to bed.

22nd. Up, and betimes to White Hall; but there the Duke of York is gone abroad a-hunting, and therefore after a little stay there I into London, with Sir H. Cholmly, talking all the way of Tangier matters, wherein I find him troubled from some reports lately from Norwood (who is his great enemy and I doubt an ill man), of some decay of the Mole, and a breach made therein by the sea to a great value. He set me down at the end of Leadenhall Street, and so I home, and after dinner, with my wife, in her morning-gown, and the two girls dressed, to Unthanke's, where my wife dresses herself, having her gown this day laced, and a new petticoat; and so is indeed very fine. And in the evening I do carry them to White Hall, and there did without much trouble get into the playhouse, there in a good place among the Ladies of Honour, and myself also sat in the pit; and there by and by come the King and Queen, and they begun "Bartholomew Fayre." But I like no play here so well as at the common playhouse; besides that, my eyes being very ill since last Sunday and this day se'nnight, with the light of the candles, I was in mighty pain to defend myself now from the light of the candles. After the play done, we met with W. Batelier and W. Hewer and Talbot Pepys, and they follow us in a hackney-coach: and we all stopped at Hercules' Pillars; and there I did give them the best supper I could, and pretty merry; and so home between eleven and twelve at night, and so to bed, mightily well pleased with this day's work.

23rd. Up: and to the Office, where all the morning, and then home, and put a mouthfull of victuals in my mouth; and by a hackney-coach followed my wife and the girls, who are gone by eleven o'clock, thinking to have seen a new play at the Duke of York's house. But I do find them staying at my tailor's, the play not being to-day, and therefore I now took them to Westminster Abbey, and there did show them all the tombs very finely, having one with us alone, there being other company this day to see the tombs, it being Shrove Tuesday; and here we did see, by particular favour, the body of Queen Katherine of Valois; and I had the upper part of her body in my hands, and I did kiss her mouth, reflecting upon it that I did kiss a Queen,

[Pepys's attachment to the fair sex extended even to a dead queen.
The record of this royal salute on his natal day is very
    characteristic. The story told him in Westminster Abbey appears to
    have been correct; for Neale informs us ("History of Westminster
    Abbey," vol. ii., p. 88) that near the south side of Henry V.'s tomb
    there was formerly a wooden chest, or coffin, wherein part of the
    skeleton and parched body of Katherine de Valois, his queen (from
    the waist upwards), was to be seen. She was interred in January,
    1457, in the Chapel of Our Lady, at the east end of this church; but
    when that building was pulled down by her grandson, Henry VII., her
    coffin was found to be decayed, and her body was taken up, and
    placed in a chest, near her first husband's tomb. "There," says
    Dart, "it hath ever since continued to be seen, the bones being
    firmly united, and thinly clothed with flesh, like scrapings of
    tanned leather." This awful spectacle of frail mortality was at
    length removed from the public gaze into St. Nicholas's Chapel, and
    finally deposited under the monument of Sir George Villiers, when
    the vault was made for the remains of Elizabeth Percy, Duchess of
    Northumberland, in December, 1776.—B.]

and that this was my birth-day, thirty-six years old, that I did first kiss a Queen. But here this man, who seems to understand well, tells me that the saying is not true that says she was never buried, for she was buried; only, when Henry the Seventh built his chapel, it was taken up and laid in this wooden coffin; but I did there see that, in it, the body was buried in a leaden one, which remains under the body to this day. Thence to the Duke of York's playhouse, and there, finding the play begun, we homeward to the Glass-House,

[Glass House Alley, Whitefriars and Blackfriars, marked the site for
    some years: The Whitefriars Glass Works of Messrs. Powell and Sons
    are on the old site, now Temple Street.]

and there shewed my cozens the making of glass, and had several things made with great content; and, among others, I had one or two singing-glasses made, which make an echo to the voice, the first that ever I saw; but so thin, that the very breath broke one or two of them. So home, and thence to Mr. Batelier's, where we supped, and had a good supper, and here was Mr. Gumbleton; and after supper some fiddles, and so to dance; but my eyes were so out of order, that I had little pleasure this night at all, though I was glad to see the rest merry, and so about midnight home and to bed.

24th. Lay long in bed, both being sleepy and my eyes bad, and myself having a great cold so as I was hardly able to speak, but, however, by and by up and to the office, and at noon home with my people to dinner, and then I to the office again, and there till the evening doing of much business, and at night my wife sends for me to W. Hewer's lodging, where I find two best chambers of his so finely furnished, and all so rich and neat, that I was mightily pleased with him and them and here only my wife, and I, and the two girls, and had a mighty neat dish of custards and tarts, and good drink and talk. And so away home to bed, with infinite content at this his treat; for it was mighty pretty, and everything mighty rich.

25th. All the morning at the office. At noon home and eat a bit myself, and then followed my wife and girls to the Duke of York's house, and there before one, but the house infinite full, where, by and by, the King and Court come, it being a new play, or an old one new vamped, by Shadwell, called "The Royall Shepherdesse;" but the silliest for words and design, and everything, that ever I saw in my whole life, there being nothing in the world pleasing in it, but a good martial dance of pikemen, where Harris and another do handle their pikes in a dance to admiration; but never less satisfied with a play in my life. Thence to the office I, and did a little business, and so home to supper with my girls, and pretty merry, only my eyes, which continue very bad, and my cold, that I cannot speak at all, do trouble me.

26th. Was forced to send my excuse to the Duke of York for my not attending him with my fellows this day because of my cold, and was the less troubled because I was thereby out of the way to offer my proposals about Pursers till the Surveyor hath delivered his notions, which he is to do to-day about something he has to offer relating to the Navy in general, which I would be glad to see and peruse before I offer what I have to say. So lay long in bed, and then up and to my office, and so to dinner, and then, though I could not speak, yet I went with my wife and girls to the King's playhouse, to shew them that, and there saw "The Faithfull Shepherdesse." But, Lord! what an empty house, there not being, as I could tell the people, so many as to make up above L10 in the whole house! The being of a new play at the other house, I suppose, being the cause, though it be so silly a play that I wonder how there should be enough people to go thither two days together, and not leave more to fill this house. The emptiness of the house took away our pleasure a great deal, though I liked it the better; for that I plainly discern the musick is the better, by how much the house the emptier. Thence home, and again to W. Hewer's, and had a pretty little treat, and spent an hour or two, my voice being wholly taken away with my cold, and so home and to bed.

27th. Up, and at the office all the morning, where I could speak but a little. At noon home to dinner, and all the afternoon till night busy at the office again, where forced to speak low and dictate. But that that troubles me most is my eyes, which are still mighty bad night and day, and so home at night to talk and sup with my cozens, and so all of us in mighty good humour to bed.

28th (Lord's day). Up, and got my wife to read to me a copy of what the Surveyor offered to the Duke of York on Friday, he himself putting it into my hands to read; but, Lord! it is a poor, silly thing ever to think to bring it in practice, in the King's Navy. It is to have the Captains to account for all stores and victuals; but upon so silly grounds, to my thinking; and ignorance of the present instructions of Officers, that I am ashamed to hear it. However, I do take a copy of it, for my future use and answering; and so to church, where, God forgive me! I did most of the time gaze on the fine milliner's wife, in Fenchurch Street, who was at our church to-day; and so home to dinner. And after dinner to write down my Journall; and then abroad by coach with my cozens, to their father's, where we are kindly received, but he is an great pain for his man Arthur, who, he fears, is now dead, having been desperately sick, and speaks so much of him that my cozen, his wife, and I did make mirth of it, and call him Arthur O'Bradly. After staying here a little, and eat and drank, and she gave me some ginger-bread made in cakes, like chocolate, very good, made by a friend, I carried him and her to my cozen Turner's, where we staid, expecting her coming from church; but she coming not, I went to her husband's chamber in the Temple, and thence fetched her, she having been there alone ever since sermon staying till the evening to walk home on foot, her horses being ill. This I did, and brought her home. And after talking there awhile, and agreeing to be all merry at my house on Tuesday next, I away home; and there spent the evening talking and reading, with my wife and Mr. Pelling, and yet much troubled with my cold, it hardly suffering me to speak, we to bed.

MARCH 1668-1669

March 1st. Up, and to White Hall to the Committee of Tangier, but it did not meet. But here I do hear first that my Lady Paulina Montagu did die yesterday; at which I went to my Lord's lodgings, but he is shut up with sorrow, and so not to be spoken with: and therefore I returned, and to Westminster Hall, where I have not been, I think, in some months. And here the Hall was very full, the King having, by Commission to some Lords this day, prorogued the Parliament till the 19th of October next: at which I am glad, hoping to have time to go over to France this year. But I was most of all surprised this morning by my Lord Bellassis, who, by appointment, met me at Auditor Wood's, at the Temple, and tells me of a duell designed between the Duke of Buckingham and my Lord Halifax, or Sir W. Coventry; the challenge being carried by Harry Saville, but prevented by my Lord Arlington, and the King told of it; and this was all the discourse at Court this day. But I, meeting Sir W. Coventry in the Duke of York's chamber, he would not own it to me, but told me that he was a man of too much peace to meddle with fighting, and so it rested: but the talk is full in the town of the business. Thence, having walked some turns with my cozen Pepys, and most people, by their discourse, believing that this Parliament will never sit more, I away to several places to look after things against to-morrow's feast, and so home to dinner; and thence, after noon, my wife and I out by hackneycoach, and spent the afternoon in several places, doing several things at the 'Change and elsewhere against to-morrow; and, among others, I did also bring home a piece of my face cast in plaister, for to make a wizard upon, for my eyes. And so home, where W. Batelier come, and sat with us; and there, after many doubts, did resolve to go on with our feast and dancing to-morrow; and so, after supper, left the maids to make clean the house, and to lay the cloth, and other things against to-morrow, and we to bed.

2nd. Up, and at the office till noon, when home, and there I find my company come, namely, Madam Turner, Dyke, The., and Betty Turner, and Mr. Bellwood, formerly their father's clerk, but now set up for himself—a conceited, silly fellow, but one they make mightily of—my cozen Roger Pepys, and his wife, and two daughters. I had a noble dinner for them, as I almost ever had, and mighty merry, and particularly myself pleased with looking on Betty Turner, who is mighty pretty. After dinner, we fell one to one talk, and another to another, and looking over my house, and closet, and things; and The. Turner to write a letter to a lady in the country, in which I did, now and then, put in half a dozen words, and sometimes five or six lines, and then she as much, and made up a long and good letter, she being mighty witty really, though troublesome-humoured with it. And thus till night, that our musick come, and the Office ready and candles, and also W. Batelier and his sister Susan come, and also Will. Howe and two gentlemen more, strangers, which, at my request yesterday, he did bring to dance, called Mr. Ireton and Mr. Starkey. We fell to dancing, and continued, only with intermission for a good supper, till two in the morning, the musick being Greeting, and another most excellent violin, and theorbo, the best in town. And so with mighty mirth, and pleased with their dancing of jigs afterwards several of them, and, among others, Betty Turner, who did it mighty prettily; and, lastly, W. Batelier's "Blackmore and Blackmore Mad;" and then to a country-dance again, and so broke up with extraordinary pleasure, as being one of the days and nights of my life spent with the greatest content; and that which I can but hope to repeat again a few times in my whole life. This done, we parted, the strangers home, and I did lodge my cozen Pepys and his wife in our blue chamber. My cozen Turner, her sister, and The., in our best chamber; Bab., Betty, and Betty Turner, in our own chamber;

and myself and my wife in the maid's bed, which is very good. Our maids in the coachman's bed; the coachman with the boy in his settlebed, and Tom where he uses to lie. And so I did, to my great content, lodge at once in my house, with the greatest ease, fifteen, and eight of them strangers of quality. My wife this day put on first her French gown, called a Sac, which becomes her very well, brought her over by W. Batelier.

3rd. Up, after a very good night's rest, and was called upon by Sir H. Cholmly, who was with me an hour, and though acquainted did not stay to talk with my company I had in the house, but away, and then I to my guests, and got them to breakfast, and then parted by coaches; and I did, in mine, carry my she-cozen Pepys and her daughters home, and there left them, and so to White Hall, where W. Hewer met me; and he and I took a turn in St. James's Park, and in the Mall did meet Sir W. Coventry and Sir J. Duncomb, and did speak with them about some business before the Lords of the Treasury; but I did find them more than usually busy, though I knew not then the reason of it, though I guess it by what followed to-morrow. Thence to Dancre's, the painter's, and there saw my picture of Greenwich, finished to my very good content, though this manner of distemper do make the figures not so pleasing as in oyle. So to Unthanke's, and there took up my wife, and carried her to the Duke of York's playhouse, and there saw an old play, the first time acted these forty years, called "The Lady's Tryall," acted only by the young people of the house; but the house very full. But it is but a sorry play, and the worse by how much my head is out of humour by being a little sleepy and my legs weary since last night. So after the play we to the New Exchange, and so called at my cozen Turner's; and there, meeting Mr. Bellwood, did hear how my Lord Mayor, being invited this day to dinner at the Reader's at the Temple, and endeavouring to carry his sword up, the students did pull it down, and forced him to go and stay all the day in a private Councillor's chamber, until the Reader himself could get the young gentlemen to dinner; and then my Lord Mayor did retreat out of the Temple by stealth, with his sword up. This do make great heat among the students; and my Lord Mayor did send to the King, and also I hear that Sir Richard Browne did cause the drums to beat for the Train-bands, but all is over, only I hear that the students do resolve to try the Charter of the City. So we home, and betimes to bed, and slept well all night.

4th. Up, and a while at the office, but thinking to have Mr. Povy's business to-day at the Committee for Tangier, I left the Board and away to White Hall, where in the first court I did meet Sir Jeremy Smith, who did tell me that Sir W. Coventry was just now sent to the Tower, about the business of his challenging the Duke of Buckingham, and so was also Harry Saville to the Gate-house; which, as [he is] a gentleman, and of the Duke of York's bedchamber, I heard afterwards that the Duke of York is mightily incensed at, and do appear very high to the King that he might not be sent thither, but to the Tower, this being done only in contempt to him. This news of Sir W. Coventry did strike me to the heart, and with reason, for by this and my Lord of Ormond's business, I do doubt that the Duke of Buckingham will be so flushed, that he will not stop at any thing, but be forced to do any thing now, as thinking it not safe to end here; and, Sir W. Coventry being gone, the King will have never a good counsellor, nor the Duke of York any sure friend to stick to him; nor any good man will be left to advise what is good. This, therefore, do heartily trouble me as any thing that ever I heard. So up into the House, and met with several people; but the Committee did not meet; and the whole House I find full of this business of Sir W. Coventry's, and most men very sensible of the cause and effects of it. So, meeting with my Lord Bellassis, he told me the particulars of this matter; that it arises about a quarrel which Sir W. Coventry had with the Duke of Buckingham about a design between the Duke and Sir Robert Howard, to bring him into a play at the King's house, which W. Coventry not enduring, did by H. Saville send a letter to the Duke of Buckingham, that he had a desire to speak with him. Upon which, the Duke of Buckingham did bid Holmes, his champion ever since my Lord Shrewsbury's business,

[Charles II. wrote to his sister (Henrietta, Duchess of Orleans), on
March 7th, 1669: "I am not sorry that Sir Will. Coventry has given
me this good occasion by sending my Lord of Buckingham a challenge
to turne him out of the Councill. I do intend to turn him allso out
of the Treasury. The truth of it is, he has been a troublesome man
in both places and I am well rid of him" (Julia Cartwright's
"Madame," 1894, p. 283).]

go to him to know the business; but H. Saville would not tell it to any but himself, and therefore did go presently to the Duke of Buckingham, and told him that his uncle Coventry was a person of honour, and was sensible of his Grace's liberty taken of abusing him, and that he had a desire of satisfaction, and would fight with him. But that here they were interrupted by my Lord Chamberlain's coming in, who was commanded to go to bid the Duke of Buckingham to come to the King, Holmes having discovered it. He told me that the King did last night, at the Council, ask the Duke of Buckingham, upon his honour, whether he had received any challenge from W. Coventry? which he confessed that he had; and then the King asking W. Coventry, he told him that he did not owne what the Duke of Buckingham had said, though it was not fit for him to give him a direct contradiction. But, being by the King put upon declaring, upon his honour, the matter, he answered that he had understood that many hard questions had upon this business been moved to some lawyers, and that therefore he was unwilling to declare any thing that might, from his own mouth, render him obnoxious to his Majesty's displeasure, and, therefore, prayed to be excused: which the King did think fit to interpret to be a confession, and so gave warrant that night for his commitment to the Tower. Being very much troubled at this, I away by coach homewards, and directly to the Tower, where I find him in one Mr. Bennet's house, son to Major Bayly, one of the Officers of the Ordnance, in the Bricke Tower:

[The Brick Tower stands on the northern wall, a little to the west
of Martin tower, with which it communicates by a secret passage.
It was the residence of the Master of the Ordnance, and Raleigh was lodged here for a time.]

where I find him busy with my Lord Halifax and his brother; so I would not stay to interrupt them, but only to give him comfort, and offer my service to him, which he kindly and cheerfully received, only owning his being troubled for the King his master's displeasure, which, I suppose, is the ordinary form and will of persons in this condition. And so I parted, with great content, that I had so earilly seen him there; and so going out, did meet Sir Jer. Smith going to meet me, who had newly been with Sir W. Coventry. And so he and I by water to Redriffe, and so walked to Deptford, where I have not been, I think, these twelve months: and there to the Treasurer's house, where the Duke of York is, and his Duchess; and there we find them at dinner in the great room, unhung; and there was with them my Lady Duchess of Monmouth, the Countess of Falmouth, Castlemayne, Henrietta Hide' (my Lady Hinchingbroke's sister), and my Lady Peterborough. And after dinner Sir Jer. Smith and I were invited down to dinner with some of the Maids of Honour, namely, Mrs. Ogle, Blake, and Howard, which did me good to have the honour to dine with, and look on; and the Mother of the Maids, and Mrs. Howard, the mother of the Maid of Honour of that name, and the Duke's housekeeper here. Here was also Monsieur Blancfort, Sir Richard Powell, Colonel Villers, Sir Jonathan Trelawny, and others. And here drank most excellent, and great variety, and plenty of wines, more than I have drank, at once, these seven years, but yet did me no great hurt. Having dined and very merry, and understanding by Blancfort how angry the Duke of York was, about their offering to send Saville to the Gate-house, among the rogues; and then, observing how this company, both the ladies and all, are of a gang, and did drink a health to the union of the two brothers, and talking of others as their enemies, they parted, and so we up; and there I did find the Dupe of York and Duchess, with all the great ladies, sitting upon a carpet, on the ground, there being no chairs, playing at "I love my love with an A, because he is so and so: and I hate him with an A, because of this and that:" and some of them, but particularly the Duchess herself, and my Lady Castlemayne, were very witty. This done, they took barge, and I with Sir J. Smith to Captain Cox's; and there to talk, and left them and other company to drink; while I slunk out to Bagwell's; and there saw her, and her mother, and our late maid Nell, who cried for joy to see me, but I had no time for pleasure then nor could stay, but after drinking I back to the yard, having a month's mind para have had a bout with Nell, which I believe I could have had, and may another time. So to Cox's, and thence walked with Sir J. Smith back to Redriffe; and so, by water home, and there my wife mighty angry for my absence, and fell mightily out, but not being certain of any thing, but thinks only that Pierce or Knepp was there, and did ask me, and, I perceive, the boy, many questions. But I did answer her; and so, after much ado, did go to bed, and lie quiet all night; but [she] had another bout with me in the morning, but I did make shift to quiet her, but yet she was not fully satisfied, poor wretch! in her mind, and thinks much of my taking so much pleasure from her; which, indeed, is a fault, though I did not design or foresee it when I went.

5th. Up, and by water to White Hall, where did a little business with the Duke of York at our usual attending him, and thence to my wife, who was with my coach at Unthanke's, though not very well of those upon her, and so home to dinner, and after dinner I to the Tower, where I find Sir W. Coventry with abundance of company with him; and after sitting awhile, and hearing some merry discourse, and, among others, of Mr. Brouncker's being this day summoned to Sir William Morton, one of the judges, to give in security for his good behaviour, upon his words the other day to Sir John Morton, a Parliamentman, at White Hall, who had heretofore spoke very highly against Brouncker in the House, I away, and to Aldgate, and walked forward towards White Chapel, till my wife overtook me with the coach, it being a mighty fine afternoon; and there we went the first time out of town with our coach and horses, and went as far as Bow, the spring beginning a little now to appear, though the way be dirty; and so, with great pleasure, with the fore-part of our coach up, we spent the afternoon. And so in the evening home, and there busy at the Office awhile, and so to bed, mightily pleased with being at peace with my poor wife, and with the pleasure we may hope to have with our coach this summer, when the weather comes to be good.

6th. Up, and to the office, where all the morning, only before the Office I stepped to Sir W. Coventry at the Tower, and there had a great deal of discourse with him; among others, of the King's putting him out of the Council yesterday, with which he is well contented, as with what else they can strip him of, he telling me, and so hath long done, that he is weary and surfeited of business; but he joins with me in his fears that all will go to naught, as matters are now managed. He told me the matter of the play that was intended for his abuse, wherein they foolishly and sillily bring in two tables like that which he hath made, with a round hole in the middle, in his closet, to turn himself in; and he is to be in one of them as master, and Sir J. Duncomb in the other, as his man or imitator: and their discourse in those tables, about the disposing of their books and papers, very foolish. But that, that he is offended with, is his being made so contemptible, as that any should dare to make a gentleman a subject for the mirth of the world: and that therefore he had told Tom Killigrew that he should tell his actors, whoever they were, that did offer at any thing like representing him, that he would not complain to my Lord Chamberlain, which was too weak, nor get him beaten, as Sir Charles Sidly is said to do, but that he would cause his nose to be cut. He told me the passage at the Council much like what my Lord Bellassis told me. He told me how that the Duke of Buckingham did himself, some time since, desire to join with him, of all men in England, and did bid him propound to himself to be Chief Minister of State, saying that he would bring it about, but that he refused to have anything to do with any faction; and that the Duke of Buckingham did, within these few days, say that, of all men in England, he would have chosen W. Coventry to have joined entire with. He tells me that he fears their prevailing against the Duke of York; and that their violence will force them to it, as being already beyond his pardon. He repeated to me many examples of challenging of Privy-Councillors and others; but never any proceeded against with that severity which he is, it never amounting to others to more than a little confinement. He tells me of his being weary of the Treasury, and of the folly, ambition, and desire of popularity of Sir Thomas Clifford; and yet the rudeness of his tongue and passions when angry. This and much more discourse being over I with great pleasure come home and to the office, where all the morning, and at noon home to dinner, and thence to the office again, where very hard at work all the afternoon till night, and then home to my wife to read to me, and to bed, my cold having been now almost for three days quite gone from me. This day my wife made it appear to me that my late entertainment this week cost me above L12, an expence which I am almost ashamed of, though it is but once in a great while, and is the end for which, in the most part, we live, to have such a merry day once or twice in a man's life.

7th (Lord's day). Up, and to the office, busy till church time, and then to church, where a dull sermon, and so home to dinner, all alone with my wife, and then to even my Journall to this day, and then to the Tower, to see Sir W. Coventry, who had H. Jermin and a great many more with him, and more, while I was there, come in; so that I do hear that there was not less than sixty coaches there yesterday, and the other day; which I hear also that there is a great exception taken at, by the King and the Duke of Buckingham, but it cannot be helped. Thence home, and with our coach out to Suffolk Street, to see my cozen Pepys, but neither the old nor young at home. So to my cozen Turner's, and there staid talking a little, and then back to Suffolk Street, where they not being yet come home I to White Hall, and there hear that there are letters come from Sir Thomas Allen, that he hath made some kind of peace with Algiers; upon which the King and Duke of York, being to go out of town to-morrow, are met at my Lord Arlington's: so I there, and by Mr. Wren was desired to stay to see if there were occasion for their speaking with me, which I did, walking without, with Charles Porter,

[Charles Porter "was the son of a prebend[ary] in Norwich, and a
'prentice boy in the city in the rebellious times. When the
committee house was blown up, he was very active in that rising, and
after the soldiers came and dispersed the rout, he, as a rat among
joint stools, shifted to and fro among the shambles, and had forty
pistols shot at him by the troopers that rode after him to kill him
[24th April, 1648]. In that distress he had the presence of mind to
catch up a little child that, during the rout, was frighted, and
stood crying in the streets, and, unobserved by the troopers, ran
away with it. The people opened a way for him, saying, 'Make room
for the poor child.' Thus he got off, and while search was made for
him in the market-place, got into the Yarmouth ferry, and at
Yarmouth took ship and went to Holland. In Holland he
trailed a pike, and was in several actions as a common soldier. At
length he kept a cavalier eating-house; but, his customers being
needy, he soon broke, and came for England, and being a genteel
youth, was taken in among the chancery clerks, and got to be under a
master. His industry was great; and he had an acquired
dexterity and skill in the forms of the court; and although he was a
bon companion, and followed much the bottle, yet he made such
dispatches as satisfied his clients, especially the clerks, who knew
where to find him. His person was florid, and speech prompt and
articulate. But his vices, in the way of women and the bottle, were
so ungoverned, as brought him to a morsel. When the Lord
Keeper North had the Seal, who from an early acquaintance had a
kindness for him which was well known, and also that he was well
heard, as they call it, business flowed in to him very fast, and yet
he could scarce keep himself at liberty to follow his business.
At the Revolution, when his interest fell from, and his debts began
to fall upon him, he was at his wits' end. His character for
fidelity, loyalty, and facetious conversation was without
exception"—Roger North's Lives of the Norths (Lord Keeper
Guilford), ed. Jessopp, vol. i., pp. 381-2. He was originally made
Lord Chancellor of Ireland in the reign of James II., during the
viceroyalty of Lord Clarendon, 1686, when he was knighted. "He
was," says Burnet, "a man of ready wit, and being poor was thought a
person fit to be made a tool of. When Clarendon was recalled,
Porter was also displaced, and Fitton was made chancellor, a man who
knew no other law than the king's pleasure" ("Own Time"). Sir
Charles Porter was again made Lord Chancellor of Ireland in 1690,

and in this same year he acted as one of the Lords Justices. This
    note of Lord Braybrooke's is retained and added to, but the
    reference may after all be to another Charles Porter. See vol.
    iii., p. 122, and vol. vi., p. 98.]

talking of a great many things: and I perceive all the world is against the Duke of Buckingham his acting thus high, and do prophesy nothing but ruin from it: But he do well observe that the church lands cannot certainly come to much, if the King shall [be] persuaded to take them; they being leased out for long leases. By and by, after two hours' stay, they rose, having, as Wren tells me, resolved upon sending six ships to the Streights forthwith, not being contented with the peace upon the terms they demand, which are, that all our ships, where any Turks or Moores shall be found slaves, shall be prizes; which will imply that they, must be searched. I hear that to-morrow the King and the Duke of York set out for Newmarket, by three in the morning; to some foot and horse-races, to be abroad ten or twelve days: So I away, without seeing the Duke of York; but Mr. Wren showed me the Order of Council about the balancing the Storekeeper's accounts, passed the Council in the very terms I drew it, only I did put in my name as he that presented the book of Hosier's preparing, and that is left out—I mean, my name—which is no great matter. So to my wife to Suffolk Streete, where she was gone, and there I found them at supper, and eat a little with them, and so home, and there to bed, my cold pretty well gone.

8th. Up, and with W. Hewer by hackney coach to White Hall, where the King and the Duke of York is gone by three in the morning, and had the misfortune to be overset with the Duke of York, the Duke of Monmouth, and the Prince, at the King's Gate' in Holborne; and the King all dirty, but no hurt. How it come to pass I know not, but only it was dark, and the torches did not, they say, light the coach as they should do. I thought this morning to have seen my Lord Sandwich before he went out of town, but I come half an hour too late; which troubles me, I having not seen him since my Lady Palls died. So W. Hewer and I to the Harp-and-Ball, to drink my morning draught, having come out in haste; and there met with King, the Parliament-man, with whom I had some impertinent talk. And so to the Privy Seal Office, to examine what records I could find there, for my help in the great business I am put upon, of defending the present constitution of the Navy; but there could not have liberty without order from him that is in present waiting, Mr. Bickerstaffe, who is out of town. This I did after I had walked to the New Exchange and there met Mr. Moore, who went with me thither, and I find him the same discontented poor man as ever. He tells me that Mr. Shepley is upon being turned away from my Lord's family, and another sent down, which I am sorry for; but his age and good fellowship have almost made him fit for nothing. Thence, at Unthanke's my wife met me, and with our coach to my cozen Turner's and there dined, and after dinner with my wife alone to the King's playhouse, and there saw "The Mocke Astrologer," which I have often seen, and but an ordinary play; and so to my cozen Turner's again, where we met Roger Pepys, his wife, and two daughters, and there staid and talked a little, and then home, and there my wife to read to me, my eyes being sensibly hurt by the too great lights of the playhouse. So to supper and to bed.

9th. Up, and to the Tower; and there find Sir W. Coventry alone, writing down his journal, which, he tells me, he now keeps of the material things; upon which I told him, and he is the only man I ever told it to, I think, that I kept it most strictly these eight or ten years; and I am sorry almost that I told it him, it not being necessary, nor may be convenient to have it known. Here he showed me the petition he had sent to the King by my Lord Keeper, which was not to desire any admittance to employment, but submitting himself therein humbly to his Majesty; but prayed the removal of his displeasure, and that he might be set free. He tells me that my Lord Keeper did acquaint the King with the substance of it, not shewing him the petition; who answered, that he was disposing of his employments, and when that was done, he might be led to discharge him: and this is what he expects, and what he seems to desire. But by this discourse he was pleased to take occasion to shew me and read to me his account, which he hath kept by him under his own hand, of all his discourse, and the King's answers to him, upon the great business of my Lord Clarendon, and how he had first moved the Duke of York with it twice, at good distance, one after another, but without success; shewing me thereby the simplicity and reasons of his so doing, and the manner of it; and the King's accepting it, telling him that he was not satisfied in his management, and did discover some dissatisfaction against him for his opposing the laying aside of my Lord Treasurer, at Oxford, which was a secret the King had not discovered. And really I was mighty proud to be privy to this great transaction, it giving me great conviction of the noble nature and ends of Sir W. Coventry in it, and considerations in general of the consequences of great men's actions, and the uncertainty of their estates, and other very serious considerations. From this to other discourse, and so to the Office, where we sat all the morning, and after dinner by coach to my cozen Turner's, thinking to have taken the young ladies to a play; but The. was let blood to-day; and so my wife and I towards the King's playhouse, and by the way found Betty [Turner], and Bab., and Betty Pepys staying for us; and so took them all to see "Claricilla," which do not please me almost at all, though there are some good things in it. And so to my cozen Turner's again, and there find my Lady Mordaunt, and her sister Johnson; and by and by comes in a gentleman, Mr. Overbury, a pleasant man, who plays most excellently on the flagelette, a little one, that sounded as low as one of mine, and mighty pretty. Hence by and by away, and with my wife, and Bab. and Betty Pepys, and W. Hewer, whom

I carried all this day with me, to my cozen Stradwick's, where I have not been ever since my brother Tom died, there being some difference between my father and them, upon the account of my cozen Scott; and I was glad of this opportunity of seeing them, they being good and substantial people, and kind, and here met my cozen Roger and his wife, and my cozen Turner, and here, which I never did before, I drank a glass, of a pint, I believe, at one draught, of the juice of oranges, of whose peel they make comfits; and here they drink the juice as wine, with sugar, and it is very fine drink; but, it being new, I was doubtful whether it might not do me hurt. Having staid a while, my wife and I back, with my cozen Turner, etc., to her house, and there we took our leaves of my cozen Pepys, who goes with his wife and two daughters for Impington tomorrow. They are very good people, and people I love, and am obliged to, and shall have great pleasure in their friendship, and particularly in hers, she being an understanding and good woman. So away home, and there after signing my letters, my eyes being bad, to supper and to bed.

10th. Up, and by hackney-coach to Auditor Beale's Office, in Holborne, to look for records of the Navy, but he was out of the way, and so forced to go next to White Hall, to the Privy Seal; and, after staying a little there, then to Westminster, where, at the Exchequer, I met with Mr. Newport and Major Halsey; and, after doing a little business with Mr. Burges, we by water to White Hall, where I made a little stop: and so with them by coach to Temple Bar, where, at the Sugar Loaf we dined, and W. Hewer with me; and there comes a companion of theirs, Colonel Vernon, I think they called him; a merry good fellow, and one that was very plain in cursing the Duke of Buckingham, and discoursing of his designs to ruin us, and that ruin must follow his counsels, and that we are an undone people. To which the others concurred, but not so plain, but all vexed at Sir W. Coventry's being laid aside: but Vernon, he is concerned, I perceive, for my Lord Ormond's being laid aside; but their company, being all old cavaliers, were very pleasant to hear how they swear and talk. But Halsey, to my content, tells me that my Lord Duke of Albemarle says that W. Coventry being gone, nothing will be well done at the Treasury, and I believe it; but they do all talk as that Duncombe, upon some pretence or other, must follow him. Thence to Auditor Beale's, his house and office, but not to be found, and therefore to the Privy Seale at White Hall, where, with W. Hewer and Mr. Gibson, who met me at the Temple, I spent the afternoon till evening looking over the books there, and did find several things to my purpose, though few of those I designed to find, the books being kept there in no method at all. Having done there, we by water home, and there find my cozen Turner and her two daughters come to see us; and there, after talking a little, I had my coach ready, and my wife and I, they going home, we out to White Chapel to take a little ayre, though yet the dirtiness of the road do prevent most of the pleasure, which should have been from this tour. So home, and my wife to read to me till supper, and to bed.

11th. Up, and to Sir W. Coventry, to the Tower, where I walked and talked with him an hour alone, from one good thing to another: who tells me that he hears that the Commission is gone down to the King, with a blank to fill, for his place in the Treasury: and he believes it will be filled with one of our Treasurers of the Navy, but which he knows not, but he believes it will be Osborne. We walked down to the Stone Walk, which is called, it seems, my Lord of Northumberland's walk, being paved by some one of that title, that was prisoner there: and at the end of it, there is a piece of iron upon the wall, with, his armes upon it, and holes to put in a peg, for every turn that they make upon that walk. So away to the Office, where busy all the morning, and so to dinner, and so very busy all the afternoon, at my Office, late; and then home tired, to supper, with content with my wife, and so to bed, she pleasing me, though I dare not own it, that she hath hired a chambermaid; but she, after many commendations, told me that she had one great fault, and that was, that she was very handsome, at which I made nothing, but let her go on; but many times to-night she took occasion to discourse of her handsomeness, and the danger she was in by taking her, and that she did doubt yet whether it would be fit for her, to take her. But I did assure her of my resolutions to have nothing to do with her maids, but in myself I was glad to have the content to have a handsome one to look on.

12th. Up, and abroad, with my own coach, to Auditor Beale's house, and thence with W. Hewer to his Office, and there with great content spent all the morning looking over the Navy accounts of several years, and the several patents of the Treasurers, which was more than I did hope to have found there. About noon I ended there, to my great content, and giving the clerks there 20s. for their trouble, and having sent for W. Howe to me to discourse with him about the Patent Office records, wherein I remembered his brother to be concerned, I took him in my coach with W. Hewer and myself towards Westminster; and there he carried me to Nott's, the famous bookbinder, that bound for my Lord Chancellor's library; and here I did take occasion for curiosity to bespeak a book to be bound, only that I might have one of his binding. Thence back to Graye's Inne: and, at the next door, at a cook's-shop of Howe's acquaintance, we bespoke dinner, it being now two o'clock; and in the meantime he carried us into Graye's Inne, to his chamber, where I never was before; and it is very pretty, and little, and neat, as he was always. And so, after a little stay, and looking over a book or two there, we carried a piece of my Lord Coke with us, and to our dinner, where, after dinner, he read at my desire a chapter in my Lord Coke about perjury, wherein I did learn a good deal touching oaths, and so away to the Patent Office; in Chancery Lane, where his brother Jacke, being newly broke by running in debt, and growing an idle rogue, he is forced to hide himself; and W. Howe do look after the Office, and here I did set a clerk to look out some things for me in their books, while W. Hewer and I to the Crowne Offices where we met with several good things that I most wanted, and did take short notes of the dockets, and so back to the Patent Office, and did the like there, and by candle-light ended. And so home, where, thinking to meet my wife with content, after my pains all this day, I find her in her closet, alone, in the dark, in a hot fit of railing against me, upon some news she has this day heard of Deb.'s living very fine, and with black spots, and speaking ill words of her mistress, which with good reason might vex her; and the baggage is to blame, but, God knows, I know nothing of her, nor what she do, nor what becomes of her, though God knows that my devil that is within me do wish that I could. Yet God I hope will prevent me therein, for I dare not trust myself with it if I should know it; but, what with my high words, and slighting it, and then serious, I did at last bring her to very good and kind terms, poor heart! and I was heartily glad of it, for I do see there is no man can be happier than myself, if I will, with her. But in her fit she did tell me what vexed me all the night, that this had put her upon putting off her handsome maid and hiring another that was full of the small pox, which did mightily vex me, though I said nothing, and do still. So down to supper, and she to read to me, and then with all possible kindness to bed.

13th. Up, and to the Tower, to see Sir W. Coventry, and with him talking of business of the Navy, all alone, an hour, he taking physic. And so away to the Office, where all the morning, and then home to dinner, with my people, and so to the Office again, and there all the afternoon till night, when comes, by mistake, my cozen Turner, and her two daughters, which love such freaks, to eat some anchovies and ham of bacon with me, instead of noon, at dinner, when I expected them. But, however, I had done my business before they come, and so was in good humour enough to be with them, and so home to them to supper, and pretty merry, being pleased to see Betty Turner, which hath something mighty pretty. But that which put me in good humour, both at noon and night, is the fancy that I am this day made a Captain of one of the King's ships, Mr. Wren having this day sent me, the Duke of York's commission to be Captain of "The Jerzy," in order to my being of a Court-martiall for examining the loss of "The Defyance," and other things; which do give me occasion of much mirth, and may be of some use to me, at least I shall get a little money by it for the time I have it; it being designed that I must really be a Captain to be able to sit in this Court. They staid till about eight at night, and then away, and my wife to read to me, and then to bed in mighty good humour, but for my eyes.

14th (Lord's day). Up, and to my office with Tom, whom I made to read to me the books of Propositions in the time of the Grand Commission, which I did read a good part of before church, and then with my wife to church, where I did see my milliner's wife come again, which pleased me; but I durst not be seen to mind her for fear of my wife's seeing me, though the woman I did never speak twenty words to, and that but only in her husband's shop. But so fearful I am of discontenting my wife, or giving her cause of jealousy. But here we heard a most excellent good sermon of Mr. Gifford's, upon the righteousness of Scribes and Pharisees. So home to dinner and to work again, and so till dinner, where W. Howe come and dined with me, and staid and read in my Lord Cooke upon his chapter of perjury again, which pleased me, and so parted, and I to my office, and there made an end of the books of Propositions, which did please me mightily to hear read, they being excellently writ and much to the purpose, and yet so as I think I shall make good use of his defence of our present constitution. About four o'clock took coach to visit my cozen Turner, and I out with her to make a visit, but the lady she went to see was abroad. So back and to talk with her and her daughters, and then home, and she and I to walk in the garden, the first time this year, the weather being mighty temperate; and then I to write down my Journall for the last week, my eyes being very bad, and therefore I forced to find a way to use by turns with my tube, one after another, and so home to supper and to bed. Before I went from my office this night I did tell Tom my resolution not to keep him after Jane was gone, but shall do well by him, which pleases him; and I think he will presently marry her, and go away out of my house with her.

15th. Up, and by water with W. Hewer to the Temple; and thence to the Rolls, where I made inquiry for several rolls, and was soon informed in the manner of it: and so spent the whole morning with W. Hewer, he taking little notes in short-hand, while I hired a clerk there to read to me about twelve or more several rolls which I did call for: and it was great pleasure to me to see the method wherein their rolls are kept; that when the Master of the Office, one Mr. Case, do call for them, who is a man that I have heretofore known by coming to my Lord of Sandwich's, he did most readily turn to them. At noon they shut up; and W. Hewer and I did walk to the Cocke, at the end of Suffolke Streete, where I never was, a great ordinary, mightily cried up, and there bespoke a pullett; which while dressing, he and I walked into St. James's Park, and thence back, and dined very handsome, with a good soup, and a pullet, for 4s. 6d. the whole. Thence back to the Rolls, and did a little more business: and so by water to White Hall, whither. I went to speak with Mr. Williamson, that if he hath any papers relating to the Navy I might see them, which he promises me: and so by water home, with great content for what I have this day found, having got almost as much as I desire of the history of the Navy, from 1618 to 1642, when the King and Parliament fell out. So home, and did get my wife to read, and so to supper and to bed.

16th. Up, and to the office, after having visited Sir W. Coventry at the Tower, and walked with him upon the Stone Walk, alone, till other company come to him, and had very good discourse with him. At noon home, where my wife and Jane gone abroad, and Tom, in order to their buying of things for their wedding, which, upon my discourse the last night, is now resolved to be done, upon the 26th of this month, the day of my solemnity for my cutting of the stone, when my cozen Turner must be with us. My wife, therefore, not at dinner; and comes to me Mr. Evelyn of Deptford, a worthy good man, and dined with me, but a bad dinner; who is grieved for, and speaks openly to me his thoughts of, the times, and our ruin approaching; and all by the folly of the King. His business to me was about some ground of his, at Deptford, next to the King's yard: and after dinner we parted. My sister Michell coming also this day to see us, whom I left there, and I away down by water with W. Hewer to Woolwich, where I have not been I think more than a year or two, and here I saw, but did not go on board, my ship "The Jerzy," she lying at the wharf under repair. But my business was to speak with Ackworth, about some old things and passages in the Navy, for my information therein, in order to my great business now of stating the history of the Navy. This I did; and upon the whole do find that the late times, in all their management, were not more husbandly than we; and other things of good content to me. His wife was sick, and so I could not see her. Thence, after seeing Mr. Sheldon, I to Greenwich by water, and there landed at the King's house, which goes on slow, but is very pretty.

[The old palace at Greenwich had just been pulled down, and a new
   building commenced by Charles II., only one wing of which was
   completed, at the expense of L36,000, under the auspices of Webb,
   Inigo Jones's kinsman and executor. In 1694 the unfinished edifice
   was granted by William and Mary to trustees for the use and service
   of a Naval Hospital; and it has been repeatedly enlarged and
   improved till it has arrived at its present splendour.—B.]

I to the Park, there to see the prospect of the hill, to judge of Dancre's picture, which he hath made thereof for me: and I do like it very well: and it is a very pretty place. Thence to Deptford, but staid not, Uthwayte being out of the way: and so home, and then to the Ship Tavern, Morrice's, and staid till W. Hewer fetched his uncle Blackburne by appointment to me, to discourse of the business of the Navy in the late times; and he did do it, by giving me a most exact account in writing, of the several turns in the Admiralty and Navy, of the persons employed therein, from the beginning of the King's leaving the Parliament, to his Son's coming in, to my great content; and now I am fully informed in all I at present desire. We fell to other talk; and I find by him that the Bishops must certainly fall, and their hierarchy; these people have got so much ground upon the King and kingdom as is not to be got again from them: and the Bishops do well deserve it. But it is all the talk, I find, that Dr. Wilkins, my friend, the Bishop of Chester, shall be removed to Winchester, and be Lord Treasurer. Though this be foolish talk, yet I do gather that he is a mighty rising man, as being a Latitudinarian, and the Duke of Buckingham his great friend. Here we staid talking till to at night, where I did never drink before since this man come to the house, though for his pretty wife's sake I do fetch my wine from this, whom I could not nevertheless get para see to-night, though her husband did seem to call for her. So parted here and I home, and to supper and to bed.

17th. Up, and by water to see Mr. Wren, and then Mr. Williamson, who did shew me the very original bookes of propositions made by the Commissioners for the Navy, in 1618, to my great content; but no other Navy papers he could now shew me. Thence to Westminster by water and to the Hall, where Mrs. Michell do surprize me with the news that Doll Lane is suddenly brought to bed at her sister's lodgings, and gives it out that she is married, but there is no such thing certainly, she never mentioning it before, but I have cause to rejoice that I have not seen her a great while, she having several times desired my company, but I doubt to an evil end. Thence to the Exchequer, where W. Hewer come to me, and after a little business did go by water home, and there dined, and took my wife by a hackney to the King's playhouse, and saw "The Coxcomb," the first time acted, but an old play, and a silly one, being acted only by the young people. Here met cozen Turner and The. So parted there from them, and home by coach and to my letters at the office, where pretty late, and so to supper and to bed.

18th. Up, and to see Sir W. Coventry, and walked with him a good while in the Stone Walk: and brave discourse about my Lord Chancellor, and his ill managements and mistakes, and several things of the Navy, and thence to the office, where we sat all the morning, and so home to dinner, where my wife mighty finely dressed, by a maid that she hath taken, and is to come to her when Jane goes; and the same she the other day told me of, to be so handsome. I therefore longed to see her, but did not till after dinner, that my wife and I going by coach, she went with us to Holborne, where we set her down. She is a mighty proper maid, and pretty comely, but so so; but hath a most pleasing tone of voice, and speaks handsomely, but hath most great hands, and I believe ugly; but very well dressed, and good clothes, and the maid I believe will please me well enough. Thence to visit Ned Pickering and his lady, and Creed and his wife, but the former abroad, and the latter out of town, gone to my Lady Pickering's in Northamptonshire, upon occasion of the late death of their brother, Oliver Pickering, a youth, that is dead of the smallpox. So my wife and I to Dancre's to see the pictures; and thence to Hyde Park, the first time we were there this year, or ever in our own coach, where with mighty pride rode up and down, and many coaches there; and I thought our horses and coach as pretty as any there, and observed so to be by others. Here staid till night, and so home, and to the office, where busy late, and so home to supper and to bed, with great content, but much business in my head of the office, which troubles me.

19th. Up, and by water to White Hall, there to the Lords of the Treasury, and did some business, and here Sir Thomas Clifford did speak to me, as desirous that I would some time come and confer with him about the Navy, which I am glad of, but will take the direction of the Duke of York before I do it, though I would be glad to do something to secure myself, if I could, in my employment. Thence to the plaisterer's, and took my face, and my Lord Duke of Albemarle's, home with me by coach, they being done to my mind; and mighty glad I am of understanding this way of having the pictures of any friends. At home to dinner, where Mr. Sheres dined with us, but after dinner I left him and my wife, and with Commissioner Middleton and Kempthorne to a Court-martiall, to which, by virtue of my late Captainship, I am called, the first I was ever at; where many Commanders, and Kempthorne president. Here was tried a difference between Sir L. Van Hemskirke, the Dutch Captain who commands "The Nonsuch," built by his direction, and his Lieutenant; a drunken kind of silly business. We ordered the Lieutenant to ask him pardon, and have resolved to lay before the Duke of York what concerns the Captain, which was striking of his Lieutenant and challenging him to fight, which comes not within any article of the laws martiall. But upon discourse the other day with Sir W. Coventry, I did advise Middleton, and he and I did forbear to give judgment, but after the debate did withdraw into another cabin, the Court being held in one of the yachts, which was on purpose brought up over against St. Katharine's, it being to be feared that this precedent of our being made Captains, in order to the trying of the loss of "The Defyance," wherein we are the proper persons to enquire into the want of instructions while ships do lie in harbour, evil use might be hereafter made of the precedent by putting the Duke of Buckingham, or any of these rude fellows that now are uppermost, to make packed Courts, by Captains made on purpose to serve their turns. The other cause was of the loss of "The Providence" at Tangier, where the Captain's being by chance on shore may prove very inconvenient to him, for example's sake, though the man be a good man, and one whom, for Norwood's sake, I would be kind to; but I will not offer any thing to the excusing such a miscarriage. He is at present confined, till he can bring better proofs on his behalf of the reasons of his being on shore. So Middleton and I away to the Office; and there I late busy, making my people, as I have done lately, to read Mr. Holland's' Discourse of the Navy, and what other things I can get to inform me fully in all; and here late, about eight at night, comes Mr. Wren to me, who had been at the Tower to Coventry. He come only to see how matters go, and tells me, as a secret, that last night the Duke of York's closet was broken open, and his cabinets, and shut again, one of them that the rogue that did it hath left plate and a watch behind him, and therefore they fear that it was only for papers, which looks like a very malicious business in design, to hurt the Duke of York; but they cannot know that till the Duke of York comes to town about the papers, and therefore make no words of it. He gone, I to work again, and then to supper at home, and to bed.

20th. Up, and to the Tower, to W. Coventry, and there walked with him alone, on the Stone Walk, till company come to him; and there about the business of the Navy discoursed with him, and about my Lord Chancellor and Treasurer; that they were against the war [with the Dutch] at first, declaring, as wise men and statesmen, at first to the King, that they thought it fit to have a war with them at some time or other, but that it ought not to be till we found the Crowns of Spain and France together by the Bares, the want of which did ruin our war. But then he told me that, a great deal before the war, my Lord Chancellor did speak of a war with some heat, as a thing to be desired, and did it upon a belief that he could with his speeches make the Parliament give what money he pleased, and do what he would, or would make the King desire; but he found himself soon deceived of the Parliament, they having a long time before his removal been cloyed with his speeches and good words, and were come to hate him. Sir W. Coventry did tell me it, as the wisest thing that ever was said to the King by any statesman of his time, and it was by my Lord Treasurer that is dead, whom, I find, he takes for a very great statesman—that when the King did shew himself forward for passing the Act of Indemnity, he did advise the King that he would hold his hand in doing it, till he had got his power restored, that had been diminished by the late times, and his revenue settled in such a manner as he might depend on himself, without resting upon Parliaments,—and then pass it. But my Lord Chancellor, who thought he could have the command of Parliaments for ever, because for the King's sake they were awhile willing to grant all the King desired, did press for its being done; and so it was, and the King from that time able to do nothing with the Parliament almost. Thence to the office, where sat all the forenoon, and then home to dinner, and so to the office, where late busy, and so home, mightily pleased with the news brought me to-night, that the King and Duke of York are come back this afternoon, and no sooner come, but a warrant was sent to the Tower for the releasing Sir W. Coventry; which do put me in some hopes that there may be, in this absence, some accommodation made between the Duke of York and the Duke of Buckingham and; Arlington. So home, to supper, and to bed.

21st (Lord's day). Up, and by water over to Southwarke; and then, not getting a boat, I forced to walk to Stangate; and so over to White Hall, in a scull; where up to the Duke of York's dressing-room, and there met Harry Saville, and understand that Sir W. Coventry is come to his house last night. I understand by Mr. Wren that his friends having, by Secretary Trevor and my Lord Keeper, applied to the King upon his first coming home, and a promise made that he should be discharged this day, my Lord Arlington did anticipate them, by sending a warrant presently for his discharge which looks a little like kindness, or a desire of it; which God send! though I fear the contrary: however, my heart is glad that he is out. Thence up and down the House. Met with Mr. May, who tells me the story of his being put by Sir John Denham's place, of Surveyor of the King's Works, who it seems, is lately dead, by the unkindness of the Duke Buckingham, who hath brought in Dr. Wren: though, he tells me, he hath been his servant for twenty years together in all his wants and dangers, saving him from want of bread by his care and management, and with a promise of having his help in his advancement, and an engagement under his hand for L1000 not yet paid, and yet the Duke of Buckingham so ungrateful as to put him by: which is an ill thing, though Dr. Wren is a worthy man. But he tells me that the King is kind to him, and hath promised him a pension of L300 a-year out of the Works; which will be of more content to him than the place, which, under their present wants of money, is a place that disobliges most people, being not able to do what they desire to their lodgings. Here meeting with Sir H. Cholmly and Povy, that tell me that my Lord Middleton is resolved in the Cabal that he shall not go to Tangier; and that Sir Edward Harlow [Harley], whom I know not, is propounded to go, who was Governor of Dunkirke, and, they say, a most worthy brave man, which I shall be very glad of. So by water (H. Russell coming for me) home to dinner, where W. Howe comes to dine with me; and after dinner propounds to me my lending him L500, to help him to purchase a place—the Master of the Patent Office, of Sir Richard Piggott. I did give him a civil answer, but shall think twice of it; and the more, because of the changes we are like to have in the Navy, which will not make it fit for me to divide the little I have left more than I have done, God knowing what my condition is, I having not attended, and now not being able to examine what my state is, of my accounts, and being in the world, which troubles me mightily. He gone, I to the office to enter my journall for a week. News is lately come of the Algerines taking L3000 in money, out of one of our Company's East India ships, outward bound, which will certainly make the war last; which I am sorry for, being so poor as we are, and broken in pieces. At night my wife to read to me, and then to supper, where Pelling comes to see and sup with us, and I find that he is assisting my wife in getting a licence to our young people to be married this Lent, which is resolved shall be done upon Friday next, my great day, or feast, for my being cut of the stone. So after supper to bed, my eyes being very bad.

22nd. Up, and by water, with W. Newer, to White Hall, there to attend the Lords of the Treasury; but, before they sat, I did make a step to see Sir W. Coventry at his house, where, I bless God! he is come again; but in my way I met him, and so he took me into his coach and carried me to White Hall, and there set me down where he ought not—at least, he hath not yet leave to come, nor hath thought fit to ask it, hearing that Henry Saville is not only denied to kiss the King's hand, but the King, being asked it by the Duke of York, did deny it, and directed that the Duke shall not receive him, to wait upon him in his chamber, till further orders. Sir W. Coventry told me that he was going to visit Sir John Trevor, who hath been kind to him; and he shewed me a long list of all his friends that he must this week make visits to, that come to visit him in the Tower; and seems mighty well satisfied with his being out of business, but I hope he will not long be so; at least, I do believe that all must go to rat if the King do not come to see the want of such a servant. Thence to the Treasury-Chamber, and there all the morning to my great grief, put to do Sir G. Downing's work of dividing the Customes for this year, between the Navy, the Ordnance and Tangier: but it did so trouble my eyes, that I had rather have given L20 than have had it to do; but I did thereby oblige Sir Thomas Clifford and Sir J. Duncombe, and so am glad of the opportunity to recommend myself to the former for the latter I need not, he loving me well already. At it till noon, here being several of my brethren with me but doing nothing, but I all. But this day I did also represent to our Treasurers, which was read here, a state of the charge of the Navy, and what the expence of it this year would likely be; which is done so as it will appear well done and to my honour, for so the Lords did take it: and I oblige the Treasurers by doing it, at their request. Thence with W. Hewer at noon to Unthanke's, where my wife stays for me and so to the Cocke, where there was no room, and thence to King Street, to several cook's shops, where nothing to be had; and at last to the corner shop, going down Ivy Lane, by my Lord of Salisbury's, and there got a good dinner, my wife, and W. Newer, and I: and after dinner she, with her coach, home; and he and I to look over my papers for the East India Company, against the afternoon: which done, I with them to White Hall, and there to the Treasury-Chamber, where the East India Company and three Councillors pleaded against me alone, for three or four hours, till seven at night, before the Lords; and the Lords did give me the conquest on behalf of the King, but could not come to any conclusion, the Company being stiff: and so I think we shall go to law with them. This done, and my eyes mighty bad with this day's work, I to Mr. Wren's, and then up to the Duke of York, and there with Mr. Wren did propound to him my going to Chatham to-morrow with Commissioner Middleton, and so this week to make the pay there, and examine the business of "The Defyance" being lost, and other businesses, which I did the rather, that I might be out of the way at the wedding, and be at a little liberty myself for a day, or two, to find a little pleasure, and give my eyes a little ease. The Duke of York mightily satisfied with it; and so away home, where my wife troubled at my being so late abroad, poor woman! though never more busy, but I satisfied her; and so begun to put things in order for my journey to-morrow, and so, after supper, to bed.

23rd. Up, and to my office to do a little business there, and so, my things being all ready, I took coach with Commissioner Middleton, Captain Tinker, and Mr. Huchinson, a hackney coach, and over the bridge, and so out towards Chatham, and; dined at Dartford, where we staid an hour or two, it being a cold day; and so on, and got to Chatham just at night, with very good discourse by the way, but mostly of matters of religion, wherein Huchinson his vein lies. After supper, we fell to talk of spirits and apparitions, whereupon many pretty, particular stories were told, so as to make me almost afeard to lie alone, but for shame I could not help it; and so to bed and, being sleepy, fell soon to rest, and so rested well.

24th. Up, and walked abroad in the garden, and find that Mrs. Tooker has not any of her daughters here as I expected and so walked to the yard, leaving Middleton at the pay, and there I only walked up and down the yard, and then to the Hill-House, and there did give order for the coach to be made ready; and got Mr. Gibson, whom I carried with me, to go with me and Mr. Coney, the surgeon, towards Maydston which I had a mighty mind to see, and took occasion, in my way, at St. Margett's, to pretend to call to see Captain Allen to see whether Mrs. Jowles, his daughter, was there; and there his wife come to the door, he being at London, and through a window, I spied Jowles, but took no notice of he but made excuse till night, and then promised to come and see Mrs. Allen again, and so away, it being a mighty cold and windy, but clear day; and had the pleasure of seeing the Medway running, winding up and down mightily, and a very fine country; and I went a little out of the way to have visited Sir John Bankes, but he at London; but here I had a sight of his seat and house, the outside, which is an old abbey just like Hinchingbroke, and as good at least, and mighty finely placed by the river; and he keeps the grounds about it, and walls and the house, very handsome: I was mightily pleased with the sight of it. Thence to Maydstone, which I had a mighty mind to see, having never been there; and walked all up and down the town, and up to the top of the steeple, and had a noble view, and then down again: and in the town did see an old man beating of flax, and did step into the barn and give him money, and saw that piece of husbandry which I never saw, and it is very pretty: in the street also I did buy and send to our inne, the Bell, a dish of fresh fish. And so, having walked all round the town, and found it very pretty, as most towns I ever saw, though not very big, and people of good fashion in it, we to our inne to dinner, and had a good dinner; and after dinner a barber come to me, and there trimmed me, that I might be clean against night, to go to Mrs. Allen. And so, staying till about four o'clock, we set out, I alone in the coach going and coming; and in our way back, I 'light out of the way to see a Saxon monument,

[Kits-Cotty House, a cromlech in Aylesford parish, Kent, on a
  hillside adjacent to the river Medway, three and a half miles N. by
  W. of Maidstone. It consists of three upright stones and an
  overlying one, and forms a small chamber open in front. It is
  supposed to have been the centre of a group of monuments indicating
  the burial-place of the Belgian settlers in this part of Britain.
  Other stones of a similar character exist in the neighbourhood.]

as they say, of a King, which is three stones standing upright, and a great round one lying on them, of great bigness, although not so big as those on Salisbury Plain; but certainly it is a thing of great antiquity, and I mightily glad to see it; it is near to Aylesford, where Sir John Bankes lives. So homeward, and stopped again at Captain Allen's, and there 'light, and sent the coach and Gibson home, and I and Coney staid; and there comes to us Mrs. Jowles, who is a very fine, proper lady, as most I know, and well dressed. Here was also a gentleman, one Major Manly, and his wife, neighbours; and here we staid, and drank, and talked, and set Coney and him to play while Mrs. Jowles and I to talk, and there had all our old stories up, and there I had the liberty to salute her often, and pull off her glove, where her hand mighty moist, and she mighty free in kindness to me, and je do not at all doubt that I might have had that that I would have desired de elle had I had time to have carried her to Cobham, as she, upon my proposing it, was very willing to go, for elle is a whore, that is certain, but a very brave and comely one. Here was a pretty cozen of hers come in to supper also, of a great fortune, daughter-in-law to this Manly, mighty pretty, but had now such a cold, she could not speak. Here mightily pleased with Mrs. Jowles, and did get her to the street door, and there to her su breasts, and baiser her without any force, and credo that I might have had all else, but it was not time nor place. Here staid till almost twelve at night, and then with a lanthorn from thence walked over the fields, as dark as pitch, and mighty cold, and snow, to Chatham, and Mr. Coney with great kindness to me: and there all in bed before I come home, and so I presently to bed.

25th. Up, and by and by, about eight o'clock, come Rear-Admiral Kempthorne and seven Captains more, by the Duke of York's order, as we expected, to hold the Court-martiall about the loss of "The Defyance;" and so presently we by boat to "The Charles," which lies over against Upnor Castle, and there we fell to the business; and there I did manage the business, the Duke of York having, by special order, directed them to take the assistance of Commissioner Middleton and me, forasmuch as there might be need of advice in what relates to the government of the ships in harbour. And so I did lay the law open to them, and rattle the Master Attendants out of their wits almost; and made the trial last till seven at night, not eating a bit all the day; only when we had done examination, and I given my thoughts that the neglect of the Gunner of the ship was as great as

I thought any neglect could be, which might by the law deserve death, but Commissioner Middleton did declare that he was against giving the sentence of death, we withdrew, as not being of the Court, and so left them to do what they pleased; and, while they were debating it, the Boatswain of the ship did bring us out of the kettle a piece of hot salt beef, and some brown bread and brandy; and there we did make a little meal, but so good as I never would desire to eat better meat while I live, only I would have cleaner dishes. By and by they had done, and called us down from the quarterdeck; and there we find they do sentence that the Gunner of "The Defyance" should stand upon "The Charles" three hours with his fault writ upon his breast, and with a halter about his neck, and so be made incapable of any office. The truth is, the man do seem, and is, I believe, a good man; but his neglect, in trusting a girl to carry fire into his cabin, is not to be pardoned. This being done, we took boat and home; and there a good supper was ready for us, which should have been our dinner. The Captains, desirous to be at London, went away presently for Gravesend, to get thither by this night's tide; and so we to supper, it having been a great snowy and mighty cold, foul day; and so after supper to bed.

26th. Up, and with Middleton all the morning at the Docke, looking over the storehouses and Commissioner Pett's house, in order to Captain Cox's coming to live there in his stead, as Commissioner. But it is a mighty pretty house; and pretty to see how every thing is said to be out of repair for this new man, though L10 would put it into as good condition in every thing as it ever was in, so free every body is of the King's money. By and by to Mr. Wilson's, and there drank, but did not see his wife, nor any woman in the yard, and so to dinner at the Hill-House; and after dinner, till eight at night, close, Middleton and I, examining the business of Mr. Pett, about selling a boat, and we find him a very knave; and some other quarrels of his, wherein, to justify himself, he hath made complaints of others. This being done, we to supper, and so to talk, Commissioner Middleton being mighty good company upon a journey, and so to bed, thinking how merry my people are at this time, putting Tom and Jane to bed, being to have been married this day, it being also my feast for my being cut of the stone, but how many years I do not remember, but I think it to be about ten or eleven.

27th. Up, and did a little business, Middleton and I, then; after drinking a little buttered ale, he and Huchinson and: I took coach, and, exceeding merry in talk, to Dartford: Middleton finding stories of his own life at Barbadoes, and up and down at Venice, and elsewhere, that are mighty pretty, and worth hearing; and he is a strange good companion, and; droll upon the road, more than ever I could have thought to have been in him. Here we dined and met Captain Allen of Rochester, who dined with us, and so went on his journey homeward, and we by and by took coach again and got home about six at night, it being all the morning as cold, snowy, windy, and rainy day, as any in the whole winter past, but pretty clear in the afternoon. I find all well, but my wife abroad with Jane, who was married yesterday, and I to the office busy, till by and by my wife comes home, and so home, and there hear how merry they were yesterday, and I glad at it, they being married, it seems, very handsomely, at Islington; and dined at the old house, and lay in our blue chamber, with much company, and wonderful merry. The Turner and Mary Batelier bridesmaids, and Talbot Pepys and W. Hewer bridesmen. Anon to supper and to bed, my head a little troubled with the muchness of the business I have upon me at present. So to bed.

28th (Lord's day). Lay long talking with pleasure with my wife, and so up and to the Office with Tom, who looks mighty smug upon his marriage, as Jane also do, both of whom I did give joy, and so Tom and I at work at the Office all the morning, till dinner, and then dined, W. Batelier with us; and so after dinner to work again, and sent for Gibson, and kept him also till eight at night, doing much business. And so, that being done, and my journal writ, my eyes being very bad, and every day worse and worse, I fear: but I find it most certain that stronge drinks do make my eyes sore, as they have done heretofore always; for, when I was in the country, when my eyes were at the best, their stronge beere would make my eyes sore: so home to supper, and by and by to bed.

29th. Up, and by water to White Hall; and there to the Duke of York, to shew myself, after my journey to Chatham, but did no business to-day with him: only after gone from him, I to Sir T. Clifford's; and there, after an hour's waiting, he being alone in his closet, I did speak with him, and give him the account he gave me to draw up, and he did like it very well: and then fell to talk of the business of the Navy and giving me good words, did fall foul of the constitution [of the Board], and did then discover his thoughts, that Sir J. Minnes was too old, and so was Colonel Middleton, and that my Lord Brouncker did mind his mathematics too much. I did not give much encouragement to that of finding fault with my fellow-officers; but did stand up for the constitution, and did say that what faults there were in our Office would be found not to arise from the constitution, but from the failures of the officers in whose hands it was. This he did seem to give good ear to; but did give me of myself very good words, which pleased me well, though I shall not build upon them any thing. Thence home; and after dinner by water with Tom down to Greenwich, he reading to me all the way, coming and going, my collections out of the Duke of York's old manuscript of the Navy, which I have bound up, and do please me mightily. At Greenwich I come to Captain Cocke's, where the house full of company, at the burial of James Temple, who, it seems, hath been dead these five days here I had a very good ring, which I did give my wife as soon as I come home. I spent my time there walking in the garden, talking with James Pierce, who tells me that he is certain that the Duke of Buckingham had been with his wenches all the time that he was absent, which was all the last week, nobody knowing where he was. The great talk is of the King's being hot of late against Conventicles, and to see whether the Duke of Buckingham's being returned will turn the King, which will make him very popular: and some think it is his plot to make the King thus, to shew his power in the making him change his mind. But Pierce did tell me that the King did certainly say, that he that took one stone from the Church, did take two from his Crown. By and by the corpse come out; and I, with Sir Richard Browne and Mr. Evelyn, in their coach to the church, where Mr. Plume preached. But I, in the midst of the sermon, did go out, and walked all alone, round to Deptford, thinking para have seen the wife of Bagwell, which I did at her door, but I could not conveniently go into her house, and so lost my labour: and so to the King's Yard, and there my boat by order met me; and home, where I made my boy to finish the my manuscript, and so to supper and to bed my new chamber-maid, that comes in the room of Jane; is come, Jane and Tom lying at their own lodging this night: the new maid's name is Matt, a proper and very comely maid. This day also our cook-maid Bridget went away, which I was sorry for; but, just at her going she was found to be a thief, and so I was the less trouble for it; but now our whole house will, in a manner, be new which, since Jane is gone, I am not at all sorry for, for that my late differences with my wife about poor Deb. will not be remembered. So to bed after supper, and to sleep with great content.

30th. Up, and to Sir W. Coventry, to see and discourse with him; and he tells me that he hath lately been with my Lord Keeper, and had much discourse about the Navy; and particularly he tells me that he finds they are divided touching me and my Lord Brouncker; some are for removing; and some for keeping us. He told my Lord Keeper that it would cost the King L10,000 before he hath made another as fit to serve him in the Navy as I am; which, though I believe it is true, yet I am much pleased to have that character given me by W. Coventry, whatever be the success of it. But I perceive they do think that I know too much, and shall impose upon whomever shall come next, and therefore must be removed, though he tells me that Sir T. Clifford is inclined well enough to me, and Sir T. Osborne; by what I have lately done, I suppose. This news do a little trouble me, but yet, when I consider it, it is but what I ought not to be much troubled for, considering my incapacity, in regard to my eyes, to continue long at this work, and this when I think of and talk with my wife do make me the less troubled for it. After some talk of the business of the navy more with him, I away and to the Office, where all the morning; and Sir W. Pen, the first time that he hath been here since his being last sick, which, I think, is two or three months; and I think will be the last that he will be here as one of the Board, he now inviting us all to dine with him, as a parting dinner, on Thursday next, which I am glad of, I am sure; for he is a very villain. At noon home to dinner, where, and at the office, all the afternoon, troubled at what I have this morning heard, at least my mind full of thoughts upon it, and so at night after supper to bed.

31st. Up, and by water to Sir W. Coventry's, there to talk with him about business of the Navy, and received from him direction what to advise the Duke of York at this time, which was, to submit and give way to the King's naming a man or two, that the people about him have a mind should be brought into the Navy, and perhaps that may stop their fury in running further against the whole; and this, he believes, will do it. After much discourse with him, I walked out with him into St. James's Park, where, being afeard to be seen with him, he having not leave yet to kiss the King's hand, but notice taken, as I hear, of all that go to him, I did take the pretence of my attending the Tangier Committee, to take my leave, though to serve him I should, I think, stick at nothing. At the Committee, this morning, my Lord Middleton declares at last his being ready to go, as soon as ever money can be made ready to pay the garrison: and so I have orders to get money, but how soon I know not. Thence home, and there find Mr Sheres, for whom I find my moher of late to talk with mighty kindness; and particularly he hath shewn himself to be a poet, and that she do mightily value him for. He did not stay to dine with us, but we to dinner; and then, in the afternoon, my wife being very well dressed by her new maid, we abroad, to make a visit to Mrs. Pickering; but she abroad again, and so we never yet saw her. Thence to Dancre's, and there, saw our pictures which are in doing; and I did choose a view of Rome instead of Hampton Court; and mightily pleased I shall be in them. Here were Sir Charles Cotterell and his son bespeaking something; both ingenious men. Thence my wife and I to the Park; and pretty store of company; and so home with great content the month, my mind in pretty good content for all things, but the designs on foot to bring alterations in the Office, which troubles me.

APRIL 1669

April 1st. Up, and with Colonel Middleton, at the desire of Rear-Admiral Kempthorne, the President, for our assisting them, to the Court-martiall on board a yacht in the River here, to try the business of the Purser's complaints, Baker against Trevanion, his Commander, of "The Dartmouth." But, Lord! to see what wretched doings there were among all the Commanders to ruin the Purser, and defend the Captain in all his rogueries, be it to the prejudice of the King or Purser, no good man could bear! I confess I was pretty high, which did not at least the young gentlemen Commander like; and Middleton did the like. But could not bring it to any issue this day, sitting till two o'clock; and therefore we being sent for, went to Sir W. Pen's by invitation to dine; where my wife was, and my Lord Brouncker and his mistress, and Sir J. Minnes and his niece; and here a bad dinner, and little mirth, I being little pleased with my host. However, I made myself sociable; and so, after dinner, my wife and I, with my Lord Brouncker and his mistress, they set us down at my cozen Turner's, and there we staid awhile and talked; and particularly here we met with Dr. Ball, the Parson of the Temple, who did tell me a great many pretty stories about the manner of the Parsons being paid for their preaching at Paul's heretofore, and now, and the ground of the Lecture, and heretofore the names of the founders thereof, which were many, at some 5s. , some 6s. per annum towards it: and had their names read in the pulpit every sermon among those holy persons that the Church do order a collect for, giving God thanks for. By and by comes by my desire Commissioner Middleton's coach and horses for us, and we went with it towards the Park, thinking to have met The. Turner and Betty, but did not; so turned back again to their lodging, and there found them and Mr. Batelier, and there, after a little talk, we took leave, and carry Batelier home with us. So to supper, and so to bed.

2nd. Up, and by water to White Hall, and there with the Office attended the Duke of York, and staid in White Hall till about noon, and so with W. Hewer to the Cocke, and there he and I dined alone with great content, he reading to me, for my memory's sake, my late collections of the history of the Navy, that I might represent the same by and by to the Duke of York; and so, after dinner, he and I to White Hall, and there to the Duke of York's lodgings, whither he, by and by, by his appointment come: and alone with him an hour in his closet, telling him mine and W. Coventry's advice touching the present posture of the Navy, as the Duke of Buckingham and the rest do now labour to make changes therein; and that it were best for him to suffer the King to be satisfied with the bringing in of a man or two which they desire. I did also give the Duke of York a short account of the history of the Navy, as to our Office, wherewith he was very well satisfied: but I do find that he is pretty stiff against their bringing in of men against his mind, as the Treasures were, and particularly against Child's' coming in, because he is a merchant. After much discourse with him, we parted; and [he to] the Council, while I staid waiting for his telling me when I should be ready to give him a written account of the administration of the Navy. This caused me to wait the whole afternoon, till night. In the mean time, stepping to the Duchess of York's side to speak with Lady Peterborough; I did see the young Duchess,

[The Princess Mary, afterwards Queen of England.]

a little child in hanging sleeves; dance most finely, so as almost to ravish me, her ears were so good: taught by a Frenchman that did heretofore teach the King, and all the King's children, and the Queen-Mother herself, who do still dance well. Thence to the council door and Mr. Chevins took me into the back stairs, and they with his friend, Mr. Fowkes, for whom he is very solicitous in some things depending in this Office, he did make me, with some others that he took in (among others, Alderman Back well), eat a pickled herring, the largest I ever saw, and drink variety of wines till I was almost merry; but I did keep in good tune; and so, after the Council was up, I home; and there find my wife not yet come home from Deptford, she she hath been all this day to see her mother, but she come and by, and so to talk, and supper, and to bed. This night I did bring home from the King's potticary's, in White Hall by Mr. Cooling's direction, a water that he says did him mighty good for his eyes. I pray God it may do me good; but, by his description, his disease was the same as mine, and this do encourage me to use it.

3rd. Up, and to the Council of War again, with Middleton: but the proceedings of the Commanders so devilishly bad, and so professedly partial to the Captain, that I could endure it no longer, but took occasion to pretend business at the Office, and away, and Colonel Middleton with me, who was of the same mind, and resolved to declare our minds freely to the Duke of York about it. So to the office, where we sat all the morning. Then home to dinner, and so back to the office, where busy late till night, and so home to supper and to bed.

4th (Lord's day). Up, and to church, where Alderman Backewell's wife, by my invitation with my head, come up with her mother, and sat with us, and after sermon I did walk with them home, and there left them, and home to dinner, and after dinner with Sir J. Minnes and T. Middleton to White Hall, by appointment; and at my Lord Arlington's the Office did attend the King and Cabal, to discourse the further quantity of victuals fit to be declared for, which was 2,000 men for six months; and so without more ado or stay, there, hearing no news but that Sir Thomas Allen is to be expected every hour at home with his fleete, or news of his being gone back to Algier, and so home, where got my wife to read to me; and so after supper to bed. The Queen-Mother hath been of late mighty ill, and some fears of her death.

5th. Up, and by coach, it being very cold, to White Hall, expecting a meeting of Tangier, but it did not. But, however, did wait there all the morning, and, among other things, I spent a little time with Creed walking in the garden, and talking about our Office, and Child's coming in to be a Commissioner; and, being his friend, I did think he might do me a kindness to learn of him what the Duke of Buckingham and the faction do design touching me, and to instil good words concerning me, which he says, and I believe he will: and it is but necessary; for I have not a mind indeed at this time to be put out of my Office, if I can make any shift that is honourable to keep it; but I will not do it by deserting the Duke of York. At noon by appointment comes Mr. Sheres, and he and I to Unthanke's, where my wife stays for us in our coach, and Betty Turner with her; and we to the Mulberry Garden, where Sheres is to treat us with a Spanish Olio,

[An olio is a mixed dish of meat and vegetables, and, secondarily, mixture or medley.]

by a cook of his acquaintance that is there, that was with my Lord in Spain:

and without any other company, he did do it, and mighty nobly; and the Olio was indeed a very noble dish, such as I never saw better, or any more of. This, and the discourse he did give us of Spain, and description of the Escuriall, was a fine treat. So we left other good things, that would keep till night, for a collation; and, with much content, took coach again, and went five or six miles towards Branford, the Prince of Tuscany, who comes into England only to spend money and see our country, comes into the town to-day, and is much expected; and we met him, but the coach passing by apace, we could not see much of him but he seems a very jolly and good comely man. By the way, we overtook Captain Ferrers upon his fine Spanish horse, and he is a fine horse indeed; but not so good, I think, as I have seen some. He did ride by us most of the way, and with us to the Park, and there left us, where we passed the evening, and meeting The. Turner, Talbot, W. Batelier, and his sister, in a coach, we anon took them with us to the Mulberry Garden; and there, after a walk, to supper upon what was left at noon; and very good; only Mr. Sheres being taken suddenly ill for a while, did spoil our mirth; but by and by was well again, and we mighty merry: and so broke up, and left him at Charing Cross, and so calling only at my cozen Turner's, away home, mightily pleased with the day's work, and this day come another new mayd, for a middle mayd, but her name I know not yet; and, for a cookmaid, we have, ever since Bridget went, used a blackmoore of Mr. Batelier's, Doll, who dresses our meat mighty well, and we mightily pleased with her. So by and by to bed.

6th. Up, and to the Office, and thence to the Excise Office about some business, and so back to the office and sat till late, end thence to Mr. Batelier's to dinner, where my cozen Turner and both her daughters, and Talbot Pepys and my wife, and a mighty fine dinner. They at dinner before I come; and, when I had dined, I away home, and thence to White Hall, where the Board waited on the Duke of York to discourse about the disposing of Sir Thomas Allen's fleete, which is newly come home to Portsmouth; and here Middleton and I did in plain terms acquaint the Duke of York what we thought and had observed in the late Court-martiall, which the Duke did give ear to; and though he thinks not fit to revoke what is already done in this case by a Court-martiall, yet it shall bring forth some good laws in the behaviour of Captains to their under Officers for the time to come. Thence home, and there, after a while at the Office, I home, and there come home my wife, who hath been with Batelier's late, and been dancing with the company, at which I seemed a little troubled, not being sent for thither myself, but I was not much so, but went to bed well enough pleased.

7th. Up, and by coach to my cozen Turner's, and invited them to dine at the Cocke to-day, with my wife and me; and so to the Lords of the Treasury, where all the morning, and settled matters to their liking about the assignments on the Customes, between the Navy Office and Victualler, and to that end spent most of the morning there with D. Gawden, and thence took him to the Cocke, and there left him and my clerk Gibson together evening their reckonings, while I to the New Exchange to talk with Betty, my little sempstress; and so to Mrs. Turner's, to call them to dinner, but my wife not come, I back again, and was overtaken by a porter, with a message from my wife that she was ill, and could not come to us: so I back again to Mrs. Turner's, and find them gone; and so back again to the Cocke, and there find Mr. Turner, Betty, and Talbot Pepys, and they dined with myself Sir D. Gawden and Gibson, and mighty merry, this house being famous for good meat, and particularly pease-porridge and after dinner broke up, and they away; and I to the Council-Chamber, and there heard the great complaint of the City, tried against the gentlemen of the Temple, for the late riot, as they would have it, when my Lord Mayor was there. But, upon hearing the whole business, the City was certainly to blame to charge them in this manner as with a riot: but the King and Council did forbear to determine any thing it, till the other business of the title and privilege be decided which is now under dispute at law between them, whether Temple be within the liberty of the City or no. But I, sorry to see the City so ill advised as to complain in a thing where their proofs were so weak. Thence to my cousin Turner's, and thence with her and her daughters, and her sister Turner, I carrying Betty in my lap, to Talbot's chamber at the Temple, where, by agreement, the poor rogue had a pretty dish of anchovies and sweetmeats for them; and hither come Mr. Eden, who was in his mistress's disfavour ever since the other night that he come in thither fuddled, when we were there. But I did make them friends by my buffoonery, and bringing up a way of spelling their names, and making Theophila spell Lamton, which The. would have to be the name of Mr. Eden's mistress, and mighty merry we were till late, and then I by coach home, and so to bed, my wife being ill of those, but well enough pleased with my being with them. This day I do hear that Betty Turner is to be left at school at Hackney, which I am mightily pleased with; for then I shall, now and then, see her. She is pretty, and a girl for that, and her relations, I love.

8th. Up, and to White Hall, to the King's side, to find Sir T. Clifford, where the Duke of York come and found me, which I was sorry for, for fear he should think I was making friends on that side. But I did put it off the best I could, my being there: and so, by and by, had opportunity alone to shew Sir T. Clifford the fair account I had drawn up of the Customes, which he liked, and seemed mightily pleased with me; and so away to the Excise-Office, to do a little business there, and so to the Office, where all the morning. At noon home to dinner, and then to the office again till the evening, and then with my wife by coach to Islington, to pay what we owe there, for the late dinner at Jane's wedding; and so round by Kingsland and Hogsden home, pleased with my wife's singing with me, by the way, and so to the office again a little, and then home to supper and to bed. Going this afternoon through Smithfield, I did see a coach run over the coachman's neck, and stand upon it, and yet the man rose up, and was well after it, which I thought a wonder.

9th. Up, and by water to White Hall, end there, with the Board, attended the Duke of York, and Sir Thomas Allen with us (who come to town yesterday); and it is resolved another fleete shall go to the Streights forthwith, and he command it. But his coming home is mighty hardly talked on by the merchants, for leaving their ships there to the mercy of the Turks: but of this more in my Whitbooke. Thence out, and slipped out by water to Westminster Hall and there thought to have spoke with Mrs. Martin, but she was not there, nor at home. So back again, and with W. Hewer by coach home and to dinner, and then to the office, and out again with W. Hewer to the Excise-Office, and to several places; among others, to Mr. Faythorne's, to have seen an instrument which he was said to have, for drawing perspectives, but he had it not: but here I did see his work-house, and the best things of his doing he had by him, and so to other places among others to Westminster Hall, and I took occasion to make a step to Mrs. Martin's, the first time I have been with her since her husband went last to sea, which is I think a year since. But, Lord! to hear how sillily she tells the story of her sister Doll's being a widow and lately brought to bed; and her husband, one Rowland Powell, drowned, sea with her husband, but by chance dead at sea, cast When God knows she hath played the whore, and forced at this time after she was brought to bed, this story. Thence calling at several places by the home, and there to the office, and then home to supper and to bed.

10th. Up, and to the Excise-Office, and thence to White Hall a little, and so back again to the 'Change, but nobody there, it being over, and so walked home to dinner, and after dinner comes Mr. Seymour to visit me, a talking fellow: but I hear by him that Captain Trevanion do give it out every where, that I did overrule the whole Court-martiall against him, as long as I was there; and perhaps I may receive, this time, some wrong by it: but I care not, for what I did was out of my desire of doing justice. So the office, where late, and then home to supper and to bed.

11th (Lord's day. Easter day). Up, and to Church; where Alderman Backewell's wife, and mother, and boy, and another gentlewoman, did come, and sit in our pew; but no women of our own there, and so there was room enough. Our Parson made a dull sermon, and so home to dinner; and, after dinner, my wife and I out by coach, and Balty with us, to Loton, the landscape-drawer, a Dutchman, living in St. James's Market, but there saw no good pictures. But by accident he did direct us to a painter that was then in the house with him, a Dutchman, newly come over, one Evarelst, who took us to his lodging close by, and did shew us a little flowerpot of his doing, the finest thing that ever, I think, I saw in my life; the drops of dew hanging on the leaves, so as I was forced, again and again, to put my finger to it, to feel whether my eyes were deceived or no. He do ask L70 for it: I had the vanity to bid him L20; but a better picture I never saw in my whole life; and it is worth going twenty miles to see it. Thence, leaving Balty there, I took my wife to St. James's, and there carried her to the Queen's Chapel, the first time I ever did it; and heard excellent musick, but not so good as by accident I did hear there yesterday, as I went through the Park from White Hall to see Sir W. Coventry, which I have forgot to set down in my journal yesterday. And going out of the Chapel, I did see the Prince of Tuscany' come out, a comely, black, fat man, in a mourning suit; and my wife and I did see him this afternoon through a window in this Chapel. All that Sir W. Coventry yesterday did tell me new was, that the King would not yet give him leave to come to kiss his hand; and he do believe that he will not in a great while do it, till those about him shall see fit, which I am sorry for. Thence to the Park, my wife and I; and here Sir W. Coventry did first see me and my wife in a coach of our own; and so did also this night the Duke of York, who did eye my wife mightily. But I begin to doubt that my being so much seen in my own coach at this time, may be observed to my prejudice; but I must venture it now. So home, and by night home, and so to my office, and there set down my journal, with the help of my left eye through my tube, for fourteen days' past; which is so much, as, I hope, I shall not run in arrear again, but the badness of my eyes do force me to it. So home to supper and to bed.

12th. Up, and by water to White Hall, where I of the whole Office attended the Duke of York at his meeting with Sir Thomas Allen and several flag-officers, to consider of the manner of managing the war with Algiers; and, it being a thing I was wholly silent in, I did only observe; and find that; their manner of discourse on this weighty affair was very mean and disorderly, the Duke of York himself being the man that I thought spoke most to the purpose. Having done here, I up and down the house, talking with this man and that, and: then meeting Mr. Sheres, took him to see the fine flower-pot I saw yesterday, and did again offer L20 for it; but he [Verelst] insists upon L50. Thence I took him to St. James's, but there was no musique, but so walked to White Hall, and, by and by to my wife at Unthanke's, and with her was Jane, and so to the Cocke, where they, and I, and Sheres, and Tom dined, my wife having a great desire to eat of their soup made of pease, and dined very well, and thence by water to the Bear-Garden, and there happened to sit by Sir Fretcheville Hollis, who is still full of his vain-glorious and prophane talk. Here we saw a prize fought between a soldier and country fellow, one Warrell, who promised the least in his looks, and performed the most of valour in his boldness and evenness of mind, and smiles in all he did, that ever I saw and we were all both deceived and infinitely taken with him. He did soundly beat the soldier, and cut him over the head. Thence back to White Hall, mightily pleased, all of us, with this sight, and particularly this fellow, as a most extraordinary man for his temper and evenness in fighting. And there leaving Sheres, we by our own coach home, and after sitting an hour, thrumming upon my viall, and singing, I to bed, and left my wife to do something to a waistcoat and petticoat she is to wear to-morrow. This evening, coming home, we overtook Alderman Backewell's coach and his lady, and followed them to their house, and there made them the first visit, where they received us with extraordinary civility, and owning the obligation. But I do, contrary to my expectation, find her something a proud and vain-glorious woman, in telling the number of her servants and family and expences: he is also so, but he was ever of that strain. But here he showed me the model of his houses that he is going to build in Cornhill and Lumbard Street; but he hath purchased so much there, that it looks like a little town, and must have cost him a great deal of money.

13th. Up, and at the Office a good while, and then, my wife going down the River to spend the day with her mother at Deptford, I abroad, and first to the milliner's in Fenchurch Street, over against Rawlinson's, and there, meeting both him and her in the shop, I bought a pair of gloves, and fell to talk, and found so much freedom that I stayed there the best part of the morning till towards noon, with great pleasure, it being a holiday, and then against my will away and to the 'Change, where I left W. Hewer, and I by hackney-coach to the Spittle, and heard a piece of a dull sermon to my Lord Mayor and Aldermen, and thence saw them all take horse and ride away, which I have not seen together many a-day; their wives also went in their coaches; and, indeed, the sight was mighty pleasing. Thence took occasion to go back to this milliner's [in Fenchurch Street], whose name I now understand to be Clerke; and there, her husband inviting me up to the balcony, to see the sight go by to dine at Clothworker's-Hall, I did go up and there saw it go by: and then; there being a good piece of cold roast beef upon the tables and one Margetts, a young merchant that lodges there, and is likely to marry a sister of hers, I staid and eat, and had much good conversation with her, who hath the vanity to talk of her great friends and father, one Wingate, near Welling;, that hath been a Parliament-man. Here also was Stapely: the rope-merchant, and dined with us; and, after spending most of the afternoon also, I away home, and there sent for W. Hewer, and he and I by water to White Hall to loop among other things, for Mr. May, to unbespeak his dining with me to-morrow. But here being in the court-yard, God would have it, I spied Deb., which made my heart and head to work, and I presently could not refrain, but sent W. Hewer away to look for Mr. Wren (W. Hewer, I perceive, did see her, but whether he did see me see her I know not, or suspect my sending him away I know not, but my heart could not hinder me), and I run after her and two women and a man, more ordinary people, and she in her old clothes, and after hunting a little, find them in the lobby of the chapel below stairs, and there I observed she endeavoured to avoid me, but I did speak to her and she to me, and did get her pour dire me ou she demeurs now, and did charge her para say nothing of me that I had vu elle, which she did promise, and so with my heart full of surprize and disorder I away, and meeting with Sir H. Cholmley walked into the Park with him and back again, looking to see if I could spy her again in the Park, but I could not. And so back to White Hall, and then back to the Park with Mr. May, but could see her, no more, and so with W. Hewer, who I doubt by my countenance might see some disorder in me, we home by water, and there I find Talbot Pepys, and Mrs. Turner, and Betty, come to invite us to dinner on Thursday; and, after drinking, I saw them to the water-side, and so back home through Crutched Friars, and there saw Mary Mercer, and put off my hat to her, on the other side of the way, but it being a little darkish she did not, I think, know me well, and so to my office to put my papers in order, they having been removed for my closet to be made clean, and so home to my wife, who is come home from Deptford. But, God forgive me, I hardly know how to put on confidence enough to speak as innocent, having had this passage to-day with Deb., though only, God knows, by accident. But my great pain is lest God Almighty shall suffer me to find out this girl, whom indeed I love, and with a bad amour, but I will pray to God to give me grace to forbear it. So home to supper, where very sparing in my discourse, not giving occasion of any enquiry where I have been to-day, or what I have done, and so without any trouble to-night more than my fear, we to bed.

14th. Up, and with W. Hewer to White Hall, and there I did speak with the Duke of York, the Council sitting in the morning, and it was to direct me to have my business ready of the Administration of the Office against Saturday next, when the King would have a hearing of it. Thence home, W. Hewer with me, and then out with my own coach to the Duke of York's play-house, and there saw "The Impertinents," a play which pleases me well still; but it is with great trouble that I now see a play, because of my eyes, the light of the candles making it very troublesome to me. After the play; my wife and I towards the Park, but it being too late we to Creed's, and there find him and her [his wife] together alone, in their new house, where I never was before, they lodging before at the next door, and a pretty house it is; but I do not see that they intend to keep any coach. Here they treat us like strangers, quite according to the fashion—nothing to drink or eat, which is a thing that will spoil our ever having any acquaintance with them; for we do continue the old freedom and kindness of England to all our friends. But they do here talk mightily of my Lady Paulina making a very good end, and being mighty religious in her lifetime; and hath left many good notes of sermons and religion; wrote with her own hand, hand, which nobody ever knew of; which I am glad of: but she was always a peevish lady. Thence home, and there to talk and to supper and to bed, all being very safe as to my seeing of poor

Deb. yesterday.

15th. Up, and to the office, and thence before the office sat to the Excise Office with W. Hewer, but found some occasion to go another way to the Temple upon business, and I by Deb.'s direction did know whither in Jewen Street to direct my hackney coachman, while I staid in the coach in Aldgate Street, to go thither just to enquire whether Mrs. Hunt, her aunt, was in town, who brought me word she was not; thought this was as much as I could do at once, and therefore went away troubled through that I could do no more but to the office I must go and did, and there all the morning, but coming thither I find Bagwell's wife, who did give me a little note into my hand, wherein I find her para invite me para meet her in Moorfields this noon, where I might speak with her, and so after the office was up, my wife being gone before by invitation to my cozen Turner's to dine, I to the place, and there, after walking up and down by the windmills, I did find her and talk with her, but it being holiday and the place full of people, we parted, leaving further discourse and doing to another time. Thence I away, and through Jewen Street, my mind, God knows, running that way, but stopped not, but going down Holborne hill, by the Conduit, I did see Deb. on foot going up the hill. I saw her, and she me, but she made no stop, but seemed unwilling to speak to me; so I away on, but then stopped and 'light, and after her and overtook her at the end of Hosier lane in Smithfield, and without standing in the street desired her to follow me, and I led her into a little blind alehouse within the walls, and there she and I alone fell to talk and baiser la and toker su mammailles, but she mighty coy, and I hope modest. I did give her in a paper 20s., and we did agree para meet again in the Hall at Westminster on Monday next; and so giving me great hopes by her carriage that she continues modest and honest, we did there part, she going home and I to Mrs. Turner's, but when I come back to the place where I left my coach it was gone, I having staid too long, which did trouble me to abuse the poor fellow, so that taking another coach I did direct him to find out the fellow and send him to me. At my cozen Turner's I find they are gone all to dinner to Povy's, and thither I, and there they were all, and W. Batelier and his sister, and had dined; but I had good things brought me, and then all up and down the house, and mightily pleased to see the fine rooms: but, the truth is, there are so many bad pictures, that to me make the good ones lose much of the pleasure in seeing them. The. and Betty Turner in new flowered tabby gowns, and so we were pretty merry, only my fear upon me for what I had newly done, do keep my content in. So, about five or six o'clock, away, and I took my wife and the two Bateliers, and carried them homeward, and W. Batelier 'lighting, I carried the women round by Islington, and so down Bishopsgate Street home, and there to talk and sup, and then to bed.

16th. Up, and to my chamber, where with Mr. Gibson all the morning, and there by noon did almost finish what I had to write about the Administration of the Office to present to the Duke of York, and my wife being gone abroad with W. Hewer, to see the new play to-day, at the Duke of York's house, "Guzman," I dined alone with my people, and in the afternoon away by coach to White Hall; and there the Office attended the Duke of York; and being despatched pretty soon, and told that we should not wait on the King, as intended, till Sunday, I thence presently to the Duke of York's playhouse, and there, in the 18d. seat, did get room to see almost three acts of the play; but it seemed to me but very ordinary. After the play done, I into the pit, and there find my wife and W. Hewer; and Sheres got to them, which, so jealous is my nature, did trouble me, though my judgment tells me there is no hurt in it, on neither side; but here I did meet with Shadwell, the poet, who, to my great wonder, do tell me that my Lord of [Orrery] did write this play, trying what he could do in comedy, since his heroique plays could do no more wonders. This do trouble me; for it is as mean a thing, and so he says, as hath been upon the stage a great while; and Harris, who hath no part in it, did come to me, and told me in discourse that he was glad of it, it being a play that will not take. Thence home, and to my business at the office, to finish it, but was in great pain about yesterday still, lest my wife should have sent her porter to enquire anything, though for my heart I cannot see it possible how anything could be discovered of it, but yet such is fear as to render me full of doubt and disgust. At night to supper and to bed.

17th. Up, and to the office, where all the morning. At noon at home to dinner, and there find Mr. Pierce, the surgeon, and he dined with us; and there hearing that "The Alchymist" was acted, we did go, and took him with us to the King's house; and it is still a good play, having not been acted for two or three years before; but I do miss Clun, for the Doctor. But more my eyes will not let me enjoy the pleasure I used to have in a play. Thence with my wife in hackney to Sir W. Coventry's, who being gone to the Park we drove after him, and there met him coming out, and followed him home, and there sent my wife to Unthanke's while I spent on hour with him reading over first my draught of the Administration of the Navy, which he do like very well; and so fell to talk of other things, and among the rest of the story of his late disgrace, and how basely and in what a mean manner the Duke of Buckingham hath proceeded against him—not like a man of honour. He tells me that the King will not give other answer about his coming to kiss his hands, than "Not yet." But he says that this that he desires, of kissing the King's hand, is only to show to the world that he is not discontented, and not in any desire to come again into play, though I do perceive that he speaks this with less earnestness than heretofore: and this, it may be, is, from what he told me lately, that the King is offended at what is talked, that he hath declared himself desirous not to have to do with any employment more. But he do tell me that the leisure he hath yet had do not at all begin to be burdensome to him, he knowing how to spend his time with content to himself; and that he hopes shortly to contract his expence, so as that he shall not be under any straits in that respect neither; and so seems to be in very good condition of content. Thence I away over the Park, it being now night, to White Hall, and there, in the Duchess's chamber, do find the Duke of York; and, upon my offer to speak with him, he did come to me, and withdrew to his closet, and there did hear and approve my paper of the Administration of the Navy, only did bid me alter these words, "upon the rupture between the late King and the Parliament," to these, "the beginning of the late Rebellion;" giving it me as but reason to shew that it was with the Rebellion that the Navy was put by out of its old good course, into that of a Commission. Having done this, we fell to other talk; he with great confidence telling me how matters go among our adversaries, in reference to the Navy, and that he thinks they do begin to flag; but then, beginning to talk in general of the excellency of old constitutions, he did bring out of his cabinet, and made me read it, an extract out of a book of my late Lord of Northumberland's, so prophetic of the business of Chatham, as is almost miraculous. I did desire, and he did give it me to copy out, which pleased me mightily, and so, it being late, I away and to my wife, and by hackney; home, and there, my eyes being weary with reading so much: but yet not so much as I was afeard they would, we home to supper and to bed.

18th (Lord's day). Up, and all the morning till 2 o'clock at my Office, with Gibson and Tom, about drawing up fair my discourse of the Administration of the Navy, and then, Mr. Spong being come to dine with me, I in to dinner, and then out to my Office again, to examine the fair draught; and so borrowing Sir J. Minnes's coach, he going with Colonel Middleton, I to White Hall, where we all met and did sign it and then to my Lord Arlington's, where the King, and the Duke of York, and Prince Rupert, as also Ormond and the two Secretaries, with my Lord Ashly and Sir T. Clifton was. And there, by and by, being called in, Mr. Williamson did read over our paper, which was in a letter to the Duke of York, bound up in a book with the Duke of York's Book of Instructions. He read it well; and, after read, we were bid to withdraw, nothing being at all said to it. And by and by we were called in again, and nothing said to that business; but another begun, about the state of this year's action, and our wants of money, as I had stated the same lately to our Treasurers; which I was bid, and did largely, and with great content, open. And having so done, we all withdrew, and left them to debate our supply of money; to which, being called in, and referred to attend on the Lords of the Treasury, we all departed. And I only staid in the House till the Council rose; and then to the Duke of York, who in the Duchess's chamber come to me, and told me that the book was there left with my Lord Arlington, for any of the Lords to view that had a mind, and to prepare and present to the King what they had to say in writing, to any part of it, which is all we can desire, and so that rested. The Duke of York then went to other talk; and by and by comes the Prince of Tuscany to visit him, and the Duchess; and I find that he do still remain incognito, and so intends to do all the time he stays here, for avoiding trouble to the King and himself, and expence also to both. Thence I to White Hall Gate, thinking to have found Sir J. Minnes's coach staying for me; but, not being there, and this being the first day of rain we have had many a day, the streets being as dusty as in summer, I forced to walk to my cozen Turner's, and there find my wife newly gone home, which vexed me, and so I, having kissed and taken leave of Betty, who goes to Putney to school to-morrow, I walked through the rain to the Temple, and there, with much ado, got a coach, and so home, and there to supper, and Pelling comes to us, and after much talk, we parted, and to bed.

19th. Up, and with Tom (whom, with his wife, I, and my wife, had this morning taken occasion to tell that I did intend to give him L40 for himself, and L20 to his wife, towards their setting out in the world, and that my wife would give her L20 more, that she might have as much to begin with as he) by coach to White Hall, and there having set him work in the Robe Chamber, to write something for me, I to Westminster Hall, and there walked from 10 o'clock to past 12, expecting to have met Deb., but whether she had been there before, and missing me went away, or is prevented in coming, and hath no mind to come to me (the last whereof, as being most pleasing, as shewing most modesty, I should be most glad of), I know not, but she not then appearing, I being tired with walking went home, and my wife being all day at Jane's, helping her, as she said, to cut out linen and other things belonging to her new condition, I after dinner out again, and, calling for my coach, which was at the coachmaker's, and hath been for these two or three days, to be new painted, and the window-frames gilt against May-day, went on with my hackney to White Hall, and thence by water to Westminster Hall, and there did beckon to Doll Lane, now Mrs. Powell, as she would have herself called, and went to her sister Martin's lodgings, the first time I have been there these eight or ten months, I think, and her sister being gone to Portsmouth to her Y husband, I did stay and talk and drink with Doll. So away:; and to White Hall, and there took my own coach, which was now come, and so away home, and there to do business, and my wife being come home we to talk and to sup, there having been nothing yet like discovery in my wife of what hath lately passed with me about Deb., and so with great content to bed

20th. Up; and to the Office, and my wife abroad with Mary Batelier, with our own coach, but borrowed Sir J Minnes's coachman, that so our own might stay at home, to attend at dinner; our family being mightily disordered by our little boy's falling sick the last night; and we fear it will prove the small-pox. At noon comes my guest, Mr. Hugh May, and with him Sir Henry Capell, my old Lord Capel's son, and

Mr. Parker; and I had a pretty dinner for them; and both before and after dinner had excellent discourse; and shewed them my closet and my Office, and the method of it to their great content; and more extraordinary, manly discourse and opportunity of shewing myself, and learning from others, I have not, in ordinary discourse, had in my life, they being all persons of worth, but especially Sir H. Capell, whose being a Parliament-man, and hearing my discourse in the Parliament-house, hath, as May tells me, given him along desire to know and discourse with me. In the afternoon we walked to the Old Artillery-Ground' near the Spitalfields, where I never was before, but now, by Captain Deane's invitation, did go to see his new gun tryed, this being the place where the Officers of the Ordnance do try all their great guns; and when we come, did find that the trial had been made; and they going away with extraordinary report of the proof of his gun, which, from the shortness and bigness, they do call Punchinello. But I desired Colonel Legg to stay and give us a sight of her performance, which he did, and there, in short, against a gun more than as long and as heavy again, and charged with as much powder again, she carried the same bullet as strong to the mark, and nearer and above the mark at a point blank than theirs, and is more easily managed, and recoyles no more than that, which is a thing so extraordinary as to be admired for the happiness of his invention, and to the great regret of the old Gunners and Officers of the Ordnance that were there, only Colonel Legg did do her much right in his report of her. And so, having seen this great and first experiment, we all parted, I seeing my guests into a hackney coach, and myself, with Captain Deane, taking a hackney coach, did go out towards Bow, and went as far as Stratford, and all the way talking of this invention, and he offering me a third of the profit of the invention; which, for aught I know, or do at present think, may prove matter considerable to us: for either the King will give him a reward for it, if he keeps it to himself, or he will give us a patent to make our profit of it: and no doubt but it will be of profit to merchantmen and others, to have guns of the same force at half the charge. This was our talk: and then to talk of other things, of the Navy in general: and, among other things, he did tell me that he do hear how the Duke of Buckingham hath a spite at me, which I knew before, but value it not: and he tells me that Sir T. Allen is not my friend; but for all this I am not much troubled, for I know myself so usefull that, as I believe, they will not part with me; so I thank God my condition is such that I can; retire, and be able to live with comfort, though not with abundance. Thus we spent the evening with extraordinary good discourse, to my great content, and so home to the Office, and there did some business, and then home, where my wife do come home, and I vexed at her staying out so late, but she tells me that she hath been at home with M. Batelier a good while, so I made nothing of it, but to supper and to bed.

21st. Up; and with my own coach as far as the Temple, and thence sent it to my cozen Turner, who, to ease her own horses, that are going with her out of town, do borrow mine to-day. So I to Auditor Wood's, and thereto meet, and met my Lord Bellassis upon some business of his accounts, and having done that did thence go to St. James's, and attended the Duke of York a little, being the first time of my waiting on him at St. James's this summer, whither he is now newly gone and thence walked to White Hall; and so, by and by, to the Council-Chamber, and heard a remarkable cause pleaded between the Farmers of the Excise of Wiltshire, in complaint against the justices of Peace of Salisbury: and Sir H. Finch was for the former. But, Lord! to see how he did with his admirable eloquence order the matter, is not to be conceived almost: so pleasant a thing it is to hear him plead. Then at noon by coach home, and thither by and by comes cozen Turner, and The., and Joyce, in their riding-clod: they being come from their lodgings to her husbands chamber, at the Temple, and there do lie, and purpose to go out of town on Friday next; and here I had a good dinner for them. After dinner by water to White Hall, where the Duke of York did meet our Office, and went with us to the Lords Commissioners of the Treasury; and there we did go over all the business of the state I had drawn up, of this year's action and expence, which I did do to their satisfaction, and convincing them of the necessity of providing more money, if possible, for us. Thence the Duke of York being gone, I did there stay walking with Sir H. Cholmly in the Court, talking of news; where he told me, that now the great design of the Duke of Buckingham is to prevent the meeting, since he cannot bring about with the King the dissolving, of this Parliament, that the King may not need it; and therefore my Lord St. Albans is hourly expected with great offers of a million of money,—[From Louis XIV. See April 28th]—to buy our breach with the Dutch: and this, they do think, may tempt the King to take the money, and thereby be out of a necessity of calling the Parliament again, which these people dare not suffer to meet again: but this he doubts, and so do I, that it will be to the ruin of the nation if we fall out with Holland. This we were discoursing when my boy comes to tell me that his mistress was at the Gate with the coach, whither I went, and there find my wife and the whole company. So she, and Mrs. Turner, and The., and Talbot, in mine: and Joyce, W. Batelier, and I, in a hackney, to Hyde Park, where I was ashamed to be seen; but mightily pleased, though troubled, with a drunken coachman that did not remember when we come to 'light, where it was that he took us up; but said at Hammersmith, and thither he was carrying of us when we come first out of the Park. So I carried them all to Hercules-Pillars, and there did treat them: and so, about ten at night, parted, and my wife, and I, and W. Batelier, home; and he gone, we to bed.

22nd. Up, and to the Office, where all the morning. At noon home to dinner, and Captain Deane with us; and very good discourse, and particularly about my getting a book for him to draw up his whole theory of shipping, which, at my desire, he hath gone far in, and hath shewn me what he hath done therein, to admiration. I did give him a Parallelogram, which he is mightily taken with; and so after dinner to the Office, where all the afternoon till night late, and then home. Vexed at my wife's not being come home, she being gone again abroad with M. Batelier, and come not home till ten at night, which vexed me, so that I to bed, and lay in pain awake till past one, and then to sleep.

23rd. Going to rise, without saying anything, my wife stopped me; and, after a little angry talk, did tell me how she spent all day yesterday with M. Batelier and her sweetheart, and seeing a play at the New Nursery, which is set up at the house in Lincoln's Inn Fields, which was formerly the King's house. So that I was mightily pleased again, and rose a with great content; and so by water to White Hall, and there to the Council-Chamber, and heard two or three causes: among others, that of the complaint of Sir Philip Howard and Watson, the inventors, as they pretend, of the business of varnishing and lackerworke, against the Company of Painters, who take upon them to do the same thing; where I saw a great instance of the weakness of a young Counsel not used to such an audience, against the Solicitor-General and two more able Counsel used to it. Though he had the right of, his side, and did prevail for what he pretended to against the rest, yet it was with much disadvantage and hazard. Here, also I heard Mr. Papillion' make his defence to the King, against some complaints of the Farmers of Excise; but it was so weak, and done only by his own seeking, that it was to his injury more than profit, and made his case the worse, being ill managed, and in a cause against the King. Thence at noon, the Council rising, I to Unthanke's, and there by agreement met my wife, and with her to the Cocke, and did give her a dinner, but yet both of us but in an ill humour, whatever was the matter with her, but thence to the King's playhouse, and saw "The Generous Portugalls," a play that pleases me better and better every time we see it; and, I thank God! it did not trouble my eyes so much as I was afeard it would. Here, by accident, we met Mr. Sheres, and yet I could not but be troubled, because my wife do so delight to talk of him, and to see him. Nevertheless, we took him with us to our mercer's, and to the Exchange, and he helped me to choose a summer-suit of coloured camelott, coat and breeches, and a flowered tabby vest very rich; and so home, where he took his leave, and down to Greenwich, where he hath some friends; and I to see Colonel Middleton, who hath been ill for a day or two, or three; and so home to supper, and to bed.

24th. Up, and to the office, where all the morning, and at noon home to dinner, Mr. Sheres dining with us by agreement; and my wife, which troubled me, mighty careful to have a handsome dinner for him; but yet I see no reason to be troubled at it, he being a very civil and worthy man, I think; but only it do seem to imply some little neglect of me. After dinner to the King's house, and there saw "The General" revived—a good play, that pleases me well, and thence, our coach coming for us, we parted and home, and I busy late at the office, and then home to supper and to bed. Well pleased to-night to have Lead, the vizard-maker, bring me home my vizard, with a tube fastened in it, which, I think, will do my business, at least in a great measure, for the easing of my eyes.

25th (Lord's day). Up, and to my Office awhile, and thither comes Lead with my vizard, with a tube fastened within both eyes; which, with the help which he prompts me to, of a glass in the tube, do content me mightily. So to church, where a stranger made a dull sermon, but I mightily pleased to looks upon Mr. Buckworth's little pretty daughters, and so home to, dinner, where W. Howe come and dined with us; and then I to my Office, he being gone, to write down my journal for the last twelve days: and did it with the help of my vizard and tube fixed to it, and do find it mighty manageable, but how helpfull to my eyes this trial will shew me. So abroad with my wife, in the afternoon, to the Park, where very much company, and the weather very pleasant. I carried my wife to the Lodge, the first time this year, and there in our coach eat a cheese-cake and drank a tankard of milk. I showed her this day also first the Prince of Tuscany, who was in the Park, and many very fine ladies, and so home, and after supper to bed.

26th. Up, having lain long, and then by coach with W. Hewer to the Excise Office, and so to Lilly's, the Varnishes; who is lately dead, and his wife and brother keep up the trade, and there I left my French prints to be put on boards:, and, while I was there, a fire burst out in a chimney of a house over against his house, but it was with a gun quickly put out. So to White Hall, and did a little business there at the Treasury chamber, and so homeward, calling at the laceman's for some lace for my new suit, and at my tailor's, and so home, where to dinner, and Mr. Sheres dined, with us, who come hither to-day to teach my wife the rules of perspective; but I think, upon trial, he thinks it too hard to teach her, being ignorant of the principles of lines. After dinner comes one Colonel Macnachan, one that I see often at Court, a Scotchman, but know him not; only he brings me a letter from my Lord Middleton, who, he says, is in great distress for L500 to relieve my Lord Morton with, but upon, what account I know not; and he would have me advance it without order upon his pay for Tangier, which I was astonished at, but had the grace to deny him with an excuse. And so he went away, leaving me a little troubled that I was thus driven, on a sudden, to do any thing herein; but Creed, coming just now to see me, he approves of what I have done. And then to talk of general matters, and, by and by, Sheres being gone, my wife, and he, and I out, and I set him down at Temple Bar, and myself and wife went down the Temple upon seeming business, only to put him off, and just at the Temple gate I spied Deb. with another gentlewoman, and Deb. winked on me and smiled, but undiscovered, and I was glad to see her. So my wife and

I to the 'Change, about things for her; and here, at Mrs. Burnett's shop, I am told by Betty, who was all undressed, of a great fire happened in Durham-Yard last night, burning the house of one Lady Hungerford, who was to come to town to it this night; and so the house is burned, new furnished, by carelessness of the girl sent to take off a candle from a bunch of candles, which she did by burning it off, and left the rest, as is supposed, on fire. The King and Court were here, it seems, and stopped the fire by blowing up of the next house. The King and Court went out of town to Newmarket this morning betimes, for a week. So home, and there to my chamber, and got my wife to read to me a little, and so to supper and to bed. Coming home this night I did call at the coachmaker's, and do resolve upon having the standards of my coach gilt with this new sort of varnish, which will come but to 40s.; and, contrary to my expectation, the doing of the biggest coach all over comes not to above L6, which is [not] very much.

27th. Up, and to the Office, where all the morning. At noon home to dinner, and then to the Office again, where the afternoon busy till late, and then home, and got my wife to read to me in the Nepotisme,

[The work here mentioned is a
bitter satire against the Court Rome,
    written in Italian, and attributed to
Gregorio Leti. It was first
    printed in 1667, without the name
or place of printer, but it is
    from the press of the Elzevirs. The
book obtained by Pepys was
    probably the anonymous English
translation, "Il Nipotismo di Roma:
    or the history of the Popes nephews
from the time of Sixtus the IV.
    to the death the last Pope Alexander
the VII. In two parts. Written
    originally Italian in the year 1667
and Englished by W. A. London,
    1669" 8vo. From this work the
word Nepotism is derived, and is
    applied to the bad practice of
statesmen, when in power, providing
    lucrative places for their relations.]

which is very pleasant, and so to supper and to bed. This afternoon was brought to me a fresh Distringas upon the score of the Tangier accounts which vexes me, though I hope it will not turn to my wrong.

28th. Up, and was called upon by Sir H. Cholmly to discourse about some accounts of his, of Tangier: and then other talk; and I find by him that it is brought almost effect ([through] the late endeavours of the Duke of York Duchess, the Queen-Mother, and my Lord St. Albans, together with some of the contrary faction, my Lord Arlington), that for a sum of money we shall enter into a league with the King of France, wherein, he says, my Lord Chancellor—[Clarendon; then an exile in France.]—is also concerned; and that he believes that, in the doing hereof, it is meant that he [Clarendon] shall come again, and that this sum of money will so help the King that he will not need the Parliament; and that, in that regard it will be forwarded by the Duke of Buckingham and his faction, who dread the Parliament. But hereby we must leave the Dutch, and that I doubt will undo us; and Sir H. Cholmly says he finds W. Coventry do think the like. Lady Castlemayne is instrumental in this matter, and, he say never more great with the King than she is now. But this a thing that will make the Parliament and kingdom mad, and will turn to our ruine: for with this money the King shall wanton away his time in pleasures, and think nothing of the main till it be too late. He gone, I to the office, where busy till noon, and then home to dinner, where W. Batelier dined with us, and pretty merry, and so I to the office again. This morning Mr. Sheres sent me, in two volumes, Mariana his History of Spaine, in Spanish, an excellent book; and I am much obliged for it to him.

29th. Up, and to the Office, where all the morning, and at noon dined at home, and then to the Office again, there to despatch as much business as I could, that I might be at liberty to-morrow to look after my many things that I have to do, against May-day. So at night home to supper and to bed.

30th. Up, and by coach to the coachmaker's: and there I do find a great many ladies sitting in the body of a coach that must be ended by to-morrow: they were my Lady Marquess of Winchester, Bellassis, and other great ladies; eating of bread and butter, and drinking ale. I to my coach, which is silvered over, but no varnish yet laid on, so I put it in a way of doing; and myself about other business, and particularly to see Sir W. Coventry, with whom I talked a good while to my great content; and so to other places-among others, to my tailor's: and then to the beltmaker's, where my belt cost me 55s., of the colour of my new suit; and here, understanding that the mistress of the house, an oldish woman in a hat hath some water good for the eyes, she did dress me, making my eyes smart most horribly, and did give me a little glass of it, which I will use, and hope it will do me good. So to the cutler's, and there did give Tom, who was with me all day a sword cost me 12s. and a belt of my owne; and set my own silver-hilt sword a-gilding against to-morrow. This morning I did visit Mr. Oldenburgh, and did see the instrument for perspective made by Dr. Wren, of which I have one making by Browne; and the sight of this do please me mightily. At noon my wife come to me at my tailor's, and I sent her home and myself and Tom dined at Hercules' Pillars; and so about our business again, and particularly to Lilly's, the varnisher about my prints, whereof some of them are pasted upon the boards, and to my full content. Thence to the frame-maker's one Morris, in Long Acre, who shewed me several forms of frames to choose by, which was pretty, in little bits of mouldings, to choose by. This done, I to my coachmaker's, and there vexed to see nothing yet done to my coach, at three in the afternoon; but I set it in doing, and stood by it till eight at night, and saw the painter varnish which is pretty to see how every doing it over do make it more and more yellow; and it dries as fast in the sun as it can be laid on almost; and most coaches are, now-a-days done so, and it is very pretty when laid on well, and not pale, as some are, even to shew the silver. Here I did make the workmen drink, and saw my coach cleaned and oyled; and, staying among poor people there in the alley, did hear them call their fat child Punch, which pleased me mightily that word being become a word of common use for all that is thick and short. At night home, and there find my wife hath been making herself clean against to-morrow; and, late as it was, I did send my coachman and horses to fetch home the coach to-night, and so we to supper, myself most weary with walking and standing so much, to see all things fine against to-morrow, and so to bed. God give a blessing to it! Meeting with Mr. Sheres, he went with me up and down to several places, and, among others, to buy a perriwig, but I bought none; and also to Dancre's, where he was about my picture of Windsor, which is mighty pretty, and so will the prospect of Rome be.

MAY 1669

May 1st. Up betimes. Called up by my tailor, and there first put on a summer suit this year; but it was not my fine one of flowered tabby vest, and coloured camelott tunique, because it was too fine with the gold lace at the hands, that I was afeard to be seen in it; but put on the stuff suit I made the last year, which is now repaired; and so did go to the Office in it, and sat all the morning, the day looking as if it would be fowle. At noon home to dinner, and there find my wife extraordinary fine, with her flowered tabby gown that she made two years ago, now laced exceeding pretty; and, indeed, was fine all over; and mighty earnest to go, though the day was very lowering; and she would have me put on my fine suit, which I did. And so anon we went alone through the town with our new liveries of serge, and the horses' manes and tails tied with red ribbons, and the standards there gilt with varnish, and all clean, and green refines, that people did mightily look upon us; and, the truth is, I did not see any coach more pretty, though more gay, than ours, all the day. But we set out, out of humour—I because Betty, whom I expected, was not come to go with us; and my wife that I would sit on the same seat with her, which she likes not, being so fine: and she then expected to meet Sheres, which we did in the Pell Mell, and, against my will, I was forced to take him into the coach, but was sullen all day almost, and little complaisant: the day also being unpleasing, though the Park full of coaches, but dusty and windy, and cold, and now and then a little dribbling rain; and, what made it worst, there were so many hackney-coaches as spoiled the sight of the gentlemen's; and so we had little pleasure. But here was W. Batelier and his sister in a borrowed coach by themselves, and I took them and we to the lodge; and at the door did give them a syllabub, and other things, cost me 12s. , and pretty merry. And so back to the coaches, and there till the evening, and then home, leaving Mr. Sheres at St. James's Gate, where he took leave of us for altogether, he; being this night to set out for Portsmouth post, in his way to Tangier, which troubled my wife mightily, who is mighty, though not, I think, too fond of him. But she was out of humour all the evening, and I vexed at her for it, and she did not rest almost all the night, so as in the night I was forced; to take her and hug her to put her to rest. So home, and after a little supper, to bed.

2nd (Lord's day). Up, and by water to White Hall, and there visit my Lord Sandwich, who, after about two months' absence at Hinchingbroke, come to town last night. I saw him, and very kind; and I am glad he is so, I having not wrote to him all the time, my eyes indeed not letting me. Here with Sir Charles Herbert [Harbord], and my Lord Hinchingbroke, and Sidney, we looked upon the picture of Tangier, designed: by Charles Herbert [Harbord], and drawn by Dancre, which my Lord Sandwich admires, as being the truest picture that ever he's saw in his life: and it is indeed very pretty, and I will be at the cost of having one of them. Thence with them to White Hall, and there walked out the sermon, with one or other; and then saw the Duke of York after sermon, and he talked to me a little; and so away back by water home, and after dinner got my wife to read, and then by coach, she and I, to the Park, and there spent the evening with much pleasure, it proving clear after a little shower, and we mighty fine as yesterday, and people mightily pleased with our coach, as I perceived; but I had not on my fine suit, being really afeard to wear it, it being so fine with the gold lace, though not gay. So home and to supper, and my wife to read, and Tom, my Nepotisme, and then to bed.

3rd. Up, and by coach to my Lord Brouncker's, where Sir G. Carteret did meet Sir J. Minnes and me, to discourse upon Mr. Deering's business, who was directed, in the time of the war, to provide provisions at Hamburgh, by Sir G. Carteret's direction; and now G. Carteret is afeard to own it, it being done without written order. But by our meeting we do all begin to recollect enough to preserve Mr. Deering, I think, which, poor silly man! I shall be glad of, it being too much he should suffer for endeavouring to serve us. Thence to St. James's, where the Duke of York was playing in the Pell Mell; and so he called me to him most part of the time that he played, which was an hour, and talked alone to me; and, among other things, tells me how the King will not yet be got to name anybody in the room of Pen, but puts it off for three or four days; from whence he do collect that they are brewing something for the Navy, but what he knows not; but I perceive is vexed that things should go so, and he hath reason; for he told me that it is likely they will do in this as in other things—resolve first, and consider it and the fitness of it afterward. Thence to White Hall, and met with Creed, and I took him to the Harp and Balls, and there drank a cup of ale, he and I alone, and discoursed of matters; and I perceive by him that he makes no doubt but that all will turn to the old religion, for these people cannot hold things in their hands, nor prevent its coming to that; and by his discourse fits himself for it, and would have my Lord Sandwich do so, too, and me. After a little talk with him, and particularly about the ruinous condition of Tangier, which I have a great mind to lay before the Duke of York, before it be too late, but dare not, because of his great kindness to Lord Middleton, we parted, and I homeward; but called at Povy's, and there he stopped me to dinner, there being Mr. Williamson, the Lieutenant of the Tower, Mr. Childe, and several others. And after dinner, Povy and I together to talk of Tangier; and he would have me move the Duke of York in it, for it concerns him particularly, more than any, as being the head of us; and I do think to do it. Thence home, and at the office busy all the afternoon, and so to supper and to bed.

4th. Up, and to the office, and then my wife being gone to see her mother at Deptford, I before the office sat went to the Excise Office, and thence being alone stepped into Duck Lane, and thence tried to have sent a porter to Deb.'s, but durst not trust him, and therefore having bought a book to satisfy the bookseller for my stay there, a 12d. book, Andronicus of Tom Fuller, I took coach, and at the end of Jewen Street next Red Cross Street I sent the coachman to her lodging, and understand she is gone for Greenwich to one Marys's, a tanner's, at which I, was glad, hoping to have opportunity to find her out; and so, in great fear of being seen, I to the office, and there all the morning, dined at home, and presently after dinner comes home my wife, who I believe is jealous of my spending the day, and I had very good fortune in being at home, for if Deb. had been to have been found it is forty to one but I had been abroad, God forgive me. So the afternoon at the office, and at night walked with my wife in the garden, and my Lord Brouncker with us, who is newly come to W. Pen's lodgings; and by and by comes Mr. Hooke; and my Lord, and he, and I into my Lord's lodgings, and there discoursed of many fine things in philosophy, to my great content, and so home to supper and to bed.

5th. Up, and thought to have gone with Lord Brouncker to Mr. Hooke this morning betimes; but my Lord is taken ill of the gout, and says his new lodgings have infected him, he never having had any symptoms of it till now. So walked to Gresham College, to tell Hooke that my Lord could not come; and so left word, he being abroad, and I to St. James's, and thence, with the Duke of York, to White Hall, where the Board waited on him all the morning: and so at noon with Sir Thomas Allen, and Sir Edward Scott, and Lord Carlingford, to the Spanish Embassador's, where I dined the first time. The Olio not so good as Sheres's. There was at the table himself and a Spanish Countess, a good, comely, and witty lady-three Fathers and us. Discourse good and pleasant. And here was an Oxford scholar in a Doctor of Law's gowne, sent from the College where the Embassador lay, when the Court was there, to salute him before his return to Spain: This man, though a gentle sort of scholar, yet sat like a fool for want of French or Spanish, but [knew] only Latin, which he spoke like an Englishman to one of the Fathers. And by and by he and I to talk, and the company very merry at my defending Cambridge against Oxford: and I made much use of my French and Spanish here, to my great content. But the dinner not extraordinary at all, either for quantity or quality. Thence home, where my wife ill of those upon the maid's bed, and troubled at my being abroad. So I to the office, and there till night, and then to her, and she read to me the Epistle of Cassandra, which is very good indeed; and the better to her, because recommended by Sheres. So to supper, and to bed.

6th. Up, and by coach to Sir W. Coventry's, but he gone out. I by water back to the Office, and there all the morning; then to dinner, and then to the Office again, and anon with my wife by coach to take the ayre, it being a noble day, as far as the Greene Man, mightily pleased with our journey, and our condition of doing it in our own coach, and so home, and to walk in the garden, and so to supper and to bed, my eyes being bad with writing my journal, part of it, to-night.

7th. Up, and by coach to W. Coventry's; and there to talk with him a great deal with great content; and so to the Duke of York, having a great mind to speak to him about Tangier; but, when I come to it, his interest for my Lord Middleton is such that I dare not. So to the Treasury chamber, and then walked home round by the Excise Office, having by private vows last night in prayer to God Almighty cleared my mind for the present of the thoughts of going to Deb. at Greenwich, which I did long after. I passed by Guildhall, which is almost finished, and saw a poor labourer carried by, I think, dead with a fall, as many there are, I hear. So home to dinner, and then to the office a little, and so to see my Lord Brouncker, who is a little ill of the gout; and there Madam Williams told me that she heard that my wife was going into France this year, which I did not deny, if I can get time, and I pray God I may. But I wondering how she come to know it, she tells me a woman that my wife spoke to for a maid, did tell her so, and that a lady that desires to go thither would be glad to go in her company. Thence with my wife abroad, with our coach, most pleasant weather; and to Hackney, and into the marshes, where I never was before, and thence round about to Old Ford and Bow; and coming through the latter home, there being some young gentlewomen at a door, and I seeming not to know who they were, my wife's jealousy told me presently that I knew well enough it was that damned place where Deb. dwelt, which made me swear very angrily that it was false, as it was, and I carried [her] back again to see the place, and it proved not so, so I continued out of humour a good while at it, she being willing to be friends, so I was by and by, saying no more of it. So home, and there met with a letter from Captain Silas Taylor, and, with it, his written copy of a play that he hath wrote, and intends to have acted.—It is called "The Serenade, or Disappointment," which I will read, not believing he can make any good of that kind. He did once offer to show Harris it, but Harris told him that he would judge by one Act whether it were good or no, which is indeed a foolish saying, and we see them out themselves in the choice of a play after they have read the whole, it being sometimes found not fit to act above three times; nay, and some that have been refused at one house is found a good one at the other. This made Taylor say he would not shew it him, but is angry, and hath carried it to the other house, and he thinks it will be acted there, though he tells me they are not yet agreed upon it. But I will find time to get it read to me, and I did get my wife to begin a little to-night in the garden, but not so much as I could make any judgment of it. So home to supper and to bed.

8th. Up, and to the Office, and there comes Lead to me, and at last my vizards are done, and glasses got to put in and out, as I will; and I think I have brought it to the utmost, both for easiness of using and benefit, that I can; and so I paid him 15s. for what he hath done now last, in the finishing them, and they, I hope, will do me a great deal of ease. At the Office all the morning, and this day, the first time, did alter my side of the table, after above eight years sitting on that next the fire. But now I am not able to bear the light of the windows in my eyes, I do begin there, and I did sit with much more content than I had done on the other side for a great while, and in winter the fire will not trouble my back. At noon home to dinner, and after dinner all the afternoon within, with Mr. Hater, Gibson, and W. Hewer, reading over and drawing up new things in the Instructions of Commanders, which will be good, and I hope to get them confirmed by the Duke of York, though I perceive nothing will effectually perfect them but to look over the whole body of the Instructions, of all the Officers of a ship, and make them all perfect together. This being done, comes my bookseller, and brings me home bound my collection of papers, about my Addresse to the Duke of York in August, which makes me glad, it being that which shall do me more right many years hence than, perhaps, all I ever did in my life: and therefore I do, both for my own and the King's sake,

value it much. By and by also comes Browne, the mathematical instrument maker, and brings me home my instrument for perspective, made according to the description of Dr. Wren's, in the late Transactions; and he hath made it, I think, very well, and that, that I believe will do the thing, and therein gives me great content; but have I fear all the content that must be received by my eyes is almost lost. So to the office, and there late at business, and then home to supper and to bed.

9th (Lord's day). Up; and, after dressing in my best suit with gold trimming, I to the Office, and there with Gibson and Tom finishing against to-morrow my notes upon Commanders' Instructions; and, when church-time, to church with my wife, leaving them at work. Dr. Mills preached a dull sermon, and so we home to dinner; and thence by coach to St. Andrew's, Holborne, thinking to have heard Dr. Stillingfleete preach, but we could not get a place, and so to St. Margaret's, Westminster, and there heard a sermon, and did get a place, the first we have heard there these many years, and here at a distance I saw Betty Michell, but she is become much a plainer woman than she was a girl. Thence towards the Park, but too soon to go in, so went on to Knightsbridge, and there eat and drank at "The World's End," where we had good things, and then back to the Park, and there till night, being fine weather, and much company, and so home, and after supper to bed. This day I first left off both my waistcoats by day, and my waistcoat by night, it being very hot weather, so hot as to make me break out, here and there, in my hands, which vexes me to see, but is good for me.

10th. Troubled, about three in the morning, with my wife's calling her maid up, and rising herself, to go with her coach abroad, to gather May-dew, which she did, and I troubled for it, for fear of any hurt, going abroad so betimes, happening to her; but I to sleep again, and she come home about six, and to bed again all well, and I up and with Mr. Gibson by coach to St. James's, and thence to White Hall,

where the Duke of York met the Office, and there discoursed of several things, particularly the Instructions of Commanders of ships. But here happened by chance a discourse of the Council of Trade, against which the Duke of York is mightily displeased, and particularly Mr. Child, against whom he speaking hardly, Captain Cox did second the Duke of York, by saying that he was talked of for an unfayre dealer with masters of ships, about freight: to which Sir T. Littleton very hotly and foolishly replied presently, that he never heard any honest man speak ill of Child; to which the Duke of York did make a smart reply, and was angry; so as I was sorry to hear it come so far, and that I, by seeming to assent to Cox, might be observed too much by Littleton, though I said nothing aloud, for this must breed great heart-burnings. After this meeting done, the Duke of York took the Treasurers into his closet to chide them, as Mr. Wren tells me; for that my Lord Keeper did last night at the Council say, when nobody was ready to say any thing against the constitution of the Navy, that he did believe the Treasurers of the Navy had something to say, which was very foul on their part, to be parties against us. They being gone, Mr. Wren [and I] took boat, thinking to dine with my Lord of Canterbury; but, when we come to Lambeth, the gate was shut, which is strictly done at twelve o'clock, and nobody comes in afterwards: so we lost our labour, and therefore back to White Hall, and thence walked my boy Jacke with me, to my Lord Crew, whom I have not seen since he was sick, which is eight months ago, I think and there dined with him: he is mightily broke. A stranger a country gentleman, was with him: and he pleased with my discourse accidentally about the decay of gentlemen's families in the country, telling us that the old rule was, that a family might remain fifty miles from London one hundred years, one hundred miles from London two hundred years, and so farther, or nearer London more or less years. He also told us that he hath heard his father say, that in his time it was so rare for a country gentleman to come to London, that, when he did come, he used to make his will before he set out. Thence: to St. James's, and there met the Duke of York, who told me, with great content, that he did now think he should master our adversaries, for that the King did tell him that he was; satisfied in the constitution of the Navy, but that it was well to give these people leave to object against it, which they having not done, he did give order to give warrant to the Duke of York to direct Sir Jeremy Smith to be a Commissioner of the Navy in the room of Pen; which, though he be an impertinent fellow, yet I am glad of it, it showing that the other side is not so strong as it was: and so, in plain terms, the Duke of York did tell me, that they were every day losing ground; and particularly that he would take care to keep out Child: at all which I am glad, though yet I dare not think myself secure, as the King may yet be wrought upon by these people to bring changes in our Office, and remove us, ere it be long. Thence I to White Hall, an there took boat to Westminster, and to Mrs. Martin's, who is not come to town from her husband at Portsmouth. So drank only at Cragg's with Doll, and so to the Swan, and there baiser a new maid that is there, and so to White Hall again, to a Committee of Tangier, where I see all things going to rack in the business of the Corporation, and consequently in the place, by Middleton's going. Thence walked a little with Creed, who tells me he hears how fine my horses and coach are, and advises me to avoid being noted for it, which I was vexed to hear taken notice of, it being what I feared and Povy told me of my gold-lace sleeves in the Park yesterday, which vexed me also, so as to resolve never to appear in Court with them, but presently to have them taken off, as it is fit I should, and so to my wife at Unthanke's, and coach, and so called at my tailor's to that purpose, and so home, and after a little walk in the garden, home to supper and to bed.

11th. My wife again up by four o'clock, to go to gather May-dew; and so back home by seven, to bed, and by and by I up and to the office, where all the morning, and dined at noon at home with my people, and so all the afternoon. In the evening my wife and I all alone, with the boy, by water, up as high as Putney almost, with the tide, and back again, neither staying going nor coming; but talking, and singing, and reading a foolish copy of verses upon my Lord Mayor's entertaining of all the bachelors, designed in praise to my Lord Mayor, and so home and to the office a little, and then home to bed, my eyes being bad. Some trouble at Court for fear of the Queen's miscarrying; she being, as they all conclude, far gone with child.

12th. Up, and to Westminster Hall, where the term is, and this the first day of my being there, and here by chance met Roger Pepys, come to town last night: I was glad to see him. After some talk with him and others, and among others Sir Charles Harbord and Sidney Montagu, the latter of whom is to set out to-morrow towards Flanders and Italy, I invited them to dine with me to-morrow, and so to Mrs. Martin's lodging, who come to town last night, and there je did hazer her, she having been a month, I think, at Portsmouth with her husband, newly come home from the Streights. But, Lord! how silly the woman talks of her great entertainment there, and how all the gentry come to visit her, and that she believes her husband is worth L6 or L700, which nevertheless I am glad of, but I doubt they will spend it a fast. Thence home, and after dinner my wife and I to the Duke of York's playhouse, and there, in the side balcony, over against the musick, did hear, but not see, a new play, the first day acted, "The Roman Virgin," an old play, and but ordinary, I thought; but the trouble of my eyes with the light of the candles did almost kill me. Thence to my Lord Sandwich's, and there had a promise from Sidney to come and dine with me to-morrow; and so my wife and I home in our coach, and there find my brother John, as I looked for, come to town from Ellington, where, among other things, he tell me the first news that my [sister Jackson] is with child, and fat gone, which I know not whether it did more trouble or please me, having no great care for my friends to have children; though I love other people's. So, glad to see him, we to supper, and so to bed.

13th. Up, and to the office, where all the morning, it being a rainy foul day. But at noon comes my Lord Hinchingbroke, and Sidney, and Sir Charles Harbord, and Roger Pepys, and dined with me; and had a good dinner, and very merry with; us all the afternoon, it being a farewell to Sidney; and so in the evening they away, and I to my business at the Office and so to supper, and talk with my brother, and so to bed.

14th. Up, and to St. James's to the Duke of York, and thence to White Hall, where we met about office business, and then at noon with Mr. Wren to Lambeth, to dinner with the Archbishop of Canterbury; the first time I was ever there and I have long longed for it; where a noble house, and well furnished with good pictures and furniture, and noble attendance in good order, and great deal of company, though an ordinary day; and exceeding great cheer, no where better, or so much, that ever I think I saw, for an ordinary table: and the Bishop mighty kind to me, particularly desiring my company another time, when less company there. Most of the company gone, and I going, I heard by a gentleman of a sermon that was to be there; and so I staid to hear it, thinking it serious, till by and by the gentleman told me it was a mockery, by one Cornet Bolton, a very gentleman-like man, that behind a chair did pray and preach like a Presbyter Scot that ever I heard in my life, with all the possible imitation in grimaces and voice. And his text about the hanging up their harps upon the willows: and a serious good sermon too, exclaiming against Bishops, and crying up of my good Lord Eglinton, a till it made us all burst; but I did wonder to have the Bishop at this time to make himself sport with things of this kind, but I perceive it was shewn him as a rarity; and he took care to have the room-door shut, but there were about twenty gentlemen there, and myself, infinitely pleased with the novelty. So over to White Hall, to a little Committee of Tangier; and thence walking in the Gallery, I met Sir Thomas Osborne, who, to my great content, did of his own accord fall into discourse with me, with so much professions of value and respect, placing the whole virtue of the Office of the Navy upon me, and that for the Comptroller's place, no man in England was fit for it but me, when Sir J. Minnes, as he says it is necessary, is removed: but then he knows not what to do for a man in my place; and in discourse, though I have no mind to the other, I did bring in Tom Hater to be the fittest man in the world for it, which he took good notice of. But in the whole I was mightily pleased, reckoning myself now fifty per cent. securer in my place than I did before think myself to be. Thence to Unthanke's, and there find my wife, but not dressed, which vexed me, because going to the Park, it being a most pleasant day after yesterday's rain, which lays all the dust, and most people going out thither, which vexed me. So home, sullen; but then my wife and I by water, with my brother, as high as Fulham, talking and singing, and playing the rogue with the Western barge-men, about the women of Woolwich, which mads them, an so back home to supper and to bed.

15th. Up, and at the Office all the morning. Dined at home and Creed with me home, and I did discourse about evening some reckonings with him in the afternoon; but I could not, for my eyes, do it, which troubled me, and vexed him that would not; but yet we were friends, I advancing him more without it, and so to walk all the afternoon together in the garden; and I perceive still he do expect a change in of matters, especially as to religion, and fits himself for it by professing himself for it in his discourse. He gone, I to my business at my Office, and so at night home to supper, and to bed.

16th (Lord's day). My wife and I at church, our pew filled with Mrs. Backewell, and six more that she brought with her, which vexed me at her confidence. Dined at home and W. Batelier with us, and I all the afternoon drawing up a foul draught of my petition to the Duke of York, about my eyes, for leave to spend three or four months out of the Office, drawing it so as to give occasion to a voyage abroad which I did, to my pretty good liking; and then with my wife to Hyde Park, where a good deal of company, and good weather, and so home to supper and to bed.

17th. Up, and to several places doing business, and the home to dinner, and then my wife and I and brother John by coach to the King's playhouse, and saw "The Spanish Curate" revived, which is a pretty good play, but my eyes troubled with seeing it, mightily. Thence carried them and Mr. Gibson, who met me at my Lord Brouncker's with a fair copy of my petition, which I thought to shew the Duke of York this night, but could not, and therefore carried them to the Park, where they had never been, and so home to supper and to bed. Great the news now of the French taking St. Domingo, in Spaniola, from the Spaniards, which troubles us, that they should have it, and have the honour of taking it, when we could not.

18th. Up, and to St. James's and other places, and then to the office, where all the morning. At noon home and dined in my wife's chamber, she being much troubled with the tooth-ake, and I staid till a surgeon of hers come, one Leeson, who hath formerly drawn her mouth, and he advised her to draw it: so I to the Office, and by and by word is come that she hath drawn it, which pleased me, it being well done. So I home, to comfort her, and so back to the office till night, busy, and so home to supper and to bed.

19th. With my coach to St. James's; and there finding the Duke of York gone to muster his men, in Hyde Park, I alone with my boy thither, and there saw more, walking out of my coach as other gentlemen did, of a soldier's trade, than ever I did in my life: the men being mighty fine, and their Commanders, particularly the Duke of Monmouth; but me-thought their trade but very easy as to the mustering of their men, and the men but indifferently ready to perform what was commanded, in the handling of their arms. Here the news was first talked of Harry Killigrew's being wounded in nine places last night, by footmen, in the highway, going from the Park in a hackney-coach towards Hammersmith, to his house at Turnham Greene: they being supposed to be my Lady Shrewsbury's men, she being by, in her coach with six horses; upon an old grudge of his saying openly that he had lain with her. Thence by and by to White Hall, and there I waited upon the King and Queen all dinner-time, in the Queen's lodgings, she being in her white pinner and apron, like a woman with child; and she seemed handsomer plain so, than dressed. And by and by, dinner done, I out, and to walk in the Gallery, for the Duke of York's coming out; and there, meeting Mr. May, he took me down about four o'clock to Mr. Chevins's lodgings, and all alone did get me a dish of cold chickens, and good wine; and I dined like a prince, being before very hungry and empty. By and by the Duke of York comes, and readily took me to his closet, and received my petition, and discoursed about my eyes, and pitied me, and with much kindness did give me his consent to be absent, and approved of my proposition to go into Holland to observe things there, of the Navy; but would first ask the King's leave, which he anon did, and did tell me that the King would be a good master to me, these were his words, about my eyes, and do like of my going into Holland, but do advise that nobody should know of my going thither, but pretend that I did go into the country somewhere, which I liked well. Glad of this, I home, and thence took out my wife, and to Mr. Holliard's about a swelling in her cheek, but he not at home, and so round by Islington and eat and drink, and so home, and after supper to bed. In discourse this afternoon, the Duke of York did tell me that he was the most amazed at one thing just now, that ever he was in his life, which was, that the Duke of Buckingham did just now come into the Queen's bed-chamber, where the King was, and much mixed company, and among others, Tom Killigrew, the father of Harry, who was last night wounded so as to be in danger of death, and his man is quite dead; and [Buckingham] there in discourse did say that he had spoke with some one that was by (which all the world must know that it must be his whore, my Lady Shrewsbury), who says that they did not mean to hurt, but beat him, and that he did run first at them with his sword; so that he do hereby clearly discover that he knows who did it, and is of conspiracy with them, being of known conspiracy with her, which the Duke of York did seem to be pleased with, and said it might, perhaps, cost him his life in the House of Lords; and I find was mightily pleased with it, saying it was the most impudent thing, as well as the most foolish, that ever he knew man do in all his life.

20th. Up and to the Office, where all the morning. At noon, the whole Office—Brouncker, J. Minnes, T. Middleton, Samuel Pepys, and Captain Cox to dine with the Parish, at the Three Tuns, this day being Ascension-day, where exceeding good discourse among the merchants, and thence back home, and after a little talk with my wife, to my office did a great deal of business, and so with my eyes might weary, and my head full of care how to get my accounts and business settled against my journey, home to supper, and bed. Yesterday, at my coming home, I found that my wife had, on a sudden, put away Matt upon some falling out, and I doubt my wife did call her ill names by my wife's own discourse; but I did not meddle to say anything upon it, but let her go, being not sorry, because now we may get one that speaks French, to go abroad with us.

21st. I waited with the Office upon the Duke of York in the morning. Dined at home, where Lewis Phillips the friend of his, dined with me. In the afternoon at the Office. In the evening visited by Roger Pepys and Philip Packer and so home.

22nd. Dined at home, the rest of the whole day at office.

23rd (Lord's day). Called up by Roger Pepys and his son who to church with me, and then home to dinner. In the afternoon carried them to Westminster, and myself to James's, where, not finding the Duke of York, back home, and with my wife spent the evening taking the ayre about Hackney, with great pleasure, and places we had never seen before.

24th. To White Hall, and there all the morning, and they home, and giving order for some business and setting my brother to making a catalogue of my books, I back again to W. Hewer to White Hall, where I attended the Duke of York and was by him led to [the King], who expressed great sense of my misfortune in my eyes, and concernment for their recovery; and accordingly signified, not only his assent to desire therein, but commanded me to give them rest summer, according to my late petition to the Duke of York. W. Hewer and I dined alone at the Swan; and thence having thus waited on the King, spent till four o'clock in St. James's Park, when I met my wife at Unthanke's, and so home.

25th. Dined at home; and the rest of the day, morning and afternoon, at the Office.

26th. To White Hall, where all the morning. Dined with Mr. Chevins, with Alderman Backewell, and Spragg. The Court full of the news from Captain Hubbert, of "The Milford," touching his being affronted in the Streights, shot at, and having eight men killed him by a French man-of-war, calling him "English dog," and commanding him to strike, which he refused, and, as knowing himself much too weak for him, made away from him. The Queen, as being supposed with child, fell ill, so as to call for Madam Nun, Mr. Chevins's sister, and one of her women, from dinner from us; this being the last day of their doubtfulness touching her being with child; and they were therein well confirmed by her Majesty's being well again before night. One Sir Edmund Bury Godfry, a woodmonger and justice of Peace in Westminster, having two days since arrested Sir Alexander Frazier for about L30 in firing, the bailiffs were apprehended, committed to the porter's lodge, and there, by the King's command, the last night severely whipped; from which the justice himself very hardly escaped, to such an unusual degree was the King moved therein. But he lies now in the lodge, justifying his act, as grounded upon the opinion of several of the judges, and, among others, my Lord Chief-Justice; which makes the King very angry with the Chief-Justice, as they say; and the justice do lie and justify his act, and says he will suffer in the cause for the people, and do refuse to receive almost any nutriment. The effects of it may be bad to the Court. Expected a meeting of Tangier this afternoon, but failed. So home, met by my wife at Unthanke's.

27th. At the office all the morning, dined at home, Mr. Hollier with me. Presented this day by Mr. Browne with a book of drawing by him, lately printed, which cost me 20s. to him. In the afternoon to the Temple, to meet with Auditor Aldworth about my interest account, but failed meeting him. To visit my cozen Creed, and found her ill at home, being with child, and looks poorly. Thence to her husband, at Gresham College, upon some occasions of Tangier; and so home, with Sir John Bankes with me, to Mark Lane.

28th. To St. James's, where the King's being with the Duke of York prevented a meeting of the Tangier Commission. But, Lord! what a deal of sorry discourse did I hear between the King and several Lords about him here! but very mean methought. So with Creed to the Excise Office, and back to White Hall, where, in the Park, Sir G. Carteret did give me an account of his discourse lately, with the Commissioners of Accounts, who except against many things, but none that I find considerable; among others, that of the Officers of the Navy selling of the King's goods, and particularly my providing him with calico flags, which having been by order, and but once, when necessity, and the King's apparent profit, justified it, as conformable to my particular duty, it will prove to my advantage that it be enquired into. Nevertheless, having this morning received from them a demand of an account of all monies within their cognizance, received and issued by me, I was willing, upon this hint, to give myself rest, by knowing whether their meaning therein might reach only to my Treasurership for Tangier, or the monies employed on this occasion. I went, therefore, to them this afternoon, to understand what monies they meant, where they answered me, by saying, "The eleven months' tax, customs, and prizemoney," without mentioning, any more than I demanding, the service they respected therein; and so, without further discourse, we parted, upon very good terms of respect, and with few words, but my mind not fully satisfied about the monies they mean. At noon Mr. Gibson and I dined at the Swan, and thence doing this at Brook house, and thence caking at the Excise Office for an account of payment of my tallies for Tangier, I home, and thence with my wife and brother spent the evening on the water, carrying our supper with us, as high as Chelsea; so home, making sport with the Westerne bargees, and my wife and I singing, to my great content.

29th. The King's birth-day. To White Hall, where all very gay; and particularly the Prince of Tuscany very fine, and is the first day of his appearing out of mourning, since he come. I heard the Bishop of Peterborough' preach but dully; but a good anthem of Pelham's. Home to dinner, and then with my wife to Hyde Park, where all the evening; great store of company, and great preparations by the Prince of Tuscany to celebrate the night with fire-works, for the King's birth-day. And so home.

30th (Whitsunday). By water to White Hall, and thence to Sir W. Coventry, where all the morning by his bed-side, he being indisposed. Our discourse was upon the notes I have lately prepared for Commanders' Instructions; but concluded that nothing will render them effectual, without an amendment in the choice of them, that they be seamen, and not gentleman above the command of the Admiral, by the greatness of their relations at Court. Thence to White Hall, and dined alone with Mr. Chevins his sister: whither by and by come in Mr. Progers and Sir Thomas Allen, and by and by fine Mrs. Wells, who is a great beauty; and there I had my full gaze upon her, to my great content, she being a woman of pretty conversation. Thence to the Duke of York, who, with the officers of the Navy, made a good entrance on my draught of my new Instructions to Commanders, as well expressing general [views] of a reformation among them, as liking of my humble offers towards it. Thence being called by my wife, Mr. Gibson and I, we to the Park, whence the rain suddenly home.

31st. Up very betimes, and so continued all the morning with W. Hewer, upon examining and stating my accounts, in order to the fitting myself to go abroad beyond sea, which the ill condition of my eyes, and my neglect for a year or two, hath kept me behindhand in, and so as to render it very difficult now, and troublesome to my mind to do it; but I this day made a satisfactory entrance therein. Dined at home, and in the afternoon by water to White Hall, calling by the way at Michell's, where I have not been many a day till just the other day, and now I met her mother there and knew her husband to be out of town. And here je did baiser elle, but had not opportunity para hazer some with her as I would have offered if je had had it. And thence had another meeting with the Duke of York, at White Hall, on yesterday's work, and made a good advance: and so, being called by my wife, we to the Park, Mary Batelier, and a Dutch gentleman, a friend of hers, being with us. Thence to "The World's End," a drinking-house by the Park; and there merry, and so home late.

And thus ends all that I doubt I shall ever be able to do with my own eyes in the keeping of my journal, I being not able to do it any longer, having done now so long as to undo my eyes almost every time that I take a pen in my hand; and, therefore, whatever comes of it, I must forbear: and, therefore, resolve, from this time forward, to have it kept by my people in long-hand, and must therefore be contented to set down no more than is fit for them and all the world to know; or, if there be any thing, which cannot be much, now my amours to Deb. are past, and my eyes hindering me in almost all other pleasures, I must endeavour to keep a margin in my book open, to add, here and there, a note in short-hand with my own hand.

And so I betake myself to that course, which is almost as much as to see myself go into my grave: for which, and all the discomforts that will accompany my being blind, the good God prepare me!

May 31, 1669.

END OF THE DIARY.

(SECOND) PREFACE

[This moved, by the editor, to the end where it seems to fit more comfortably.]

First issue of this edition June, 1896. Reprinted 1897.

In the present volume the Diary is completed, and we here take leave of a writer who has done so much to interest and enlighten successive generations of English readers, and who is now for the first time presented to the world as he really drew his own portrait day by day.

No one who has followed the daily notes of Samuel Pepys from January, 1660, to May, 1669, but must feel sincere regret at their abrupt conclusion, more particularly as the writer lays down his pen while in an unhappy temper.

It is evident from the tone of his later utterances that Pepys thought that he was going blind, a belief which was happily falsified. The holiday tour in which Charles II. and James, Duke of York, took so much interest appears to have had its desired effect in restoring the Diarist to health.

The rest of his eventful life must be sought in the history of the English Navy which he helped to form, and in his numerous letters, which on some future occasion the present editor hopes to annotate. The details to be obtained from these sources form, however, but a sorry substitute for the words written in the solitude of his office by Pepys for his own eye alone, and we cannot but feel how great is the world's loss in that he never resumed the writing of his journal. All must agree with Coleridge when he wrote on the margin of a copy of the Diary: "Truly may it be said that this was a greater and more grievous loss to the mind's eye of posterity than to the bodily organs of Pepys himself. It makes me restless and discontented to think what a Diary equal in minuteness and truth of portraiture to the preceding from 1669 to 1688 or 1690 would have been for the true causes, process and character of the Revolution."

Most works of this nature are apt to tire when they are extended over a certain length of time, but Pepys's pages are always fresh, and most readers wish for more. For himself the editor can say that each time he has read over the various proofs he has read with renewed interest, so that it is with no ordinary feelings of regret that he comes to the end of his task, and he believes that every reader will feel the same regret that he has no more to read.

In reviewing the Diary it is impossible not to notice the growth of historical interest as it proceeds. In the earlier period we find Pepys surrounded by men not otherwise known, but as the years pass, and his position becomes more assured, we find him in daily communication with the chief men of his day, and evidently every one who came in contact with him appreciated his remarkable ability. The survival of the Diary must ever remain a marvel. It could never have been intended for the reading of others, but doubtless the more elaborate portraits of persons in the later pages were intended for use when Pepys came to write his projected history of the Navy.

The only man who is uniformly spoken well of in the Diary is Sir William Coventry, and many of the characters introduced come in for severe castigation. It is therefore the more necessary to remember that many of the judgments on men were set down hastily, and would probably have been modified had occasion offered. At all events, we know that, however much he may have censured them, Pepys always helped on those who were dependent upon him.

H. R. W.

book EDITOR'S BOOKMARKS, DIARY OF SAMUEL PEPYS, 1969 N.S.

Broken sort of people, that have not much to lose

But so fearful I am of discontenting my wife

By her wedding-ring, I suppose he hath married her at last

Dine with them, at my cozen Roger's mistress's

Drawing up a foul draught of my petition to the Duke of York

Dutchmen come out of the mouth and tail of a Hamburgh sow

Fain to keep a woman on purpose at 20s. a week

Find it a base copy of a good originall, that vexed me

Found in my head and body about twenty lice, little and great

Have not much to lose, and therefore will venture all

His satisfaction is nothing worth, it being easily got

I have itched mightily these 6 or 7 days

I know I have made myself an immortal enemy by it

Lady Castlemayne is now in a higher command over the King

Last day of their doubtfulness touching her being with child

Mighty fond in the stories she tells of her son Will

Nor was there any pretty woman that I did see, but my wife

Observing my eyes to be mightily employed in the playhouse

Proud, carping, insolent, and ironically-prophane stile

Quite according to the fashion—nothing to drink or eat

She finds that I am lousy

Unquiet which her ripping up of old faults will give me

Up, and with W. Hewer, my guard, to White Hall

Weeping to myself for grief, which she discerning, come to bed

With egg to keep off the glaring of the light